Tending the Garden

Tending the Garden

A Guide To Spiritual Formation and Community Gardens

Marshall & Julia Welch

To order additional copies of this book, contact:
Xlibris Corporation
1-888-795-4274
www.Xlibris.com
Orders@Xlibris.com
121584

Contents

PART II

Starting a Church Community Garden

Dedicated to our life-long friends and spiritual gardeners
at Cottonwood Presbyterian Church
Salt Lake City, Utah.

Many thanks to Hilde Clark for her interest and to
Nancy Henderson for her sensitive eye.

Thanks also to Sam Hamilton-Poore
as he unknowingly planted the seed for this project.

Introduction

It All Began in the Garden

... and we've got to get ourselves back to the garden.
~ Joni Mitchell

It all began in the garden. The story of humanity begins in this wonderful place where all our needs were met. It was called Paradise. But now, just like then, we have become removed from the garden and all it provides, both literally and spiritually. It is time to get back to the garden.

So, imagine a patch of empty land. Looking at it, you might think to yourself, "What a great place for a garden!" You dash into the house to retrieve a lone pack of green bean seeds that has been sitting in the junk drawer of your kitchen. Upon returning to your patch of dirt, you poke a few holes into the soil to carefully place the seeds and cover them up. Pleased with yourself, you walk away picturing fresh green beans on your plate in a few weeks. A month later you return to the garden wondering what became of your vision, only to find a patch of weeds. Disappointed, you walk away.

This, of course, is a silly story, as no one would truly expect to harvest anything without tending to the garden. Yet, for many of us, we approach our spirituality in this same way. We plant ourselves in a church pew and expect to grow spiritually. Like the garden, we need to tend to our spirituality. In many respects, a garden serves as a lovely metaphor for this process.

This book has been designed to help you tend your own spiritual garden. We incorporate basic components of gardening to explore your own spirituality. Just think about gardens and gardening for a moment—what is involved?

As the opening story illustrated, gardening involves dirt and seeds. The earth is quite literally the foundation for our efforts, so making sure the soil is fertile is an important first step and on-going process. Likewise, our faith is the foundation for our spiritual growth. Planting seeds and patiently waiting for them to grow is an act of faith. Faith alone is not enough.

Additionally, we need to sustain the garden by watering it. Our spirituality also requires sustenance and nourishment. But watering is certainly not enough. We need to supplement the soil and plants with fertilizer and pull weeds that choke out the growth of the plants. Things may creep into our garden to threaten our crops. A gardener is also aware of, and responsive to, climatic conditions that may nurture or harm the produce. Finally, due to care and attention, we can harvest the fruit of our hard work. All of this serves nicely as a metaphor for tending to our spirituality.

Sam Hamilton-Poore borrowed conceptual frameworks of spirituality from the 1977 Scottish Council of Churches to characterize spirituality as . . .

a process of becoming fully human . . . to grow in compassion & sensitivity to one's own self, others, the non-human creation, and to God, who is within & beyond this totality. By this definition, then, spirituality is profoundly relational. *Christian* spirituality, in particular, is to become more fully human by being formed more and more in the image of Christ. We grow as Christians the more we are able to mirror or embody the spirit of Christ in all the various ways we relate to ourselves, others, the creation, and to God." (Hamilton-Poore, 2005, p. 85)

This little book has been designed to use the garden as a metaphor in helping you to grow in compassion and sensitivity to your self, others, God's creation, and God. You may even learn something about gardening along the way.

Part I of the book contains short devotional passages. Each passage begins with brief scripture and a quote we refer to as a "seedling for thought." A series of reflection questions are posed at the end of each passage. You can read these passage by yourself or, ideally, with others and discuss the reflection questions as a group. Look at each reflection question and respond to any or all that speak to you. If you are meeting with others, we suggest you break into smaller groups of three to four participants. Take turns sharing your response to the reflection questions for about ten to fifteen minutes each. The rest of the group should listen deeply without "cross-talk," interruption, advice giving, or problem solving. Sit in silence for about a minute before moving on to the next person in the group and repeat the process. At the end, the group is invited to notice themes and collectively identify a "take away" for the group.

Finally, Part II of this book provides some technical information on how to create and maintain a community garden, perhaps even at your own church. An important aspect of nurturing your spirituality is being in a community of faith, which is why many practice corporate worship on Sunday mornings. We invite you to consider how working with others in a garden can also provide a sense of spiritual community. Likewise, a community garden can be an important part of a congregation's ministry and mission when produce or the financial resources gained from selling the produce is shared locally with those who are hungry. The garden space itself can become a gathering place for fellowship as well as a sacred space to ponder important issues around food and faith. Organic gardening is a way to intentionally ponder and practice ecological stewardship of God's earth. Family and friends who visit your portion of the garden will see you model sustainable gardening and learn about issues they may not have even thought about. Lastly, a community garden serves as a welcoming natural chapel where one can sit and be still.

PART I

Our Spiritual Garden

Chapter 1

The Earth: Our Spiritual Foundation

Seedling for Thought

The best place to seek God is in a garden. You can dig for Him there.

~ George Bernard Shaw—*The Adventure of the Black Girl in Her Search for God* (1932)

Your garden will reveal yourself.

~ Henry Mitchell

Scripture

Matthew 13: 1-9

That same day Jesus went out of the house and sat by the lake. Such large crowds gathered around him that he got into a boat and sat in it, while all the people stood on the shore. Then he told them many things in parables, saying: "A farmer went out to sow his seed. As he was scattering the seed, some fell along the path, and the birds came and ate it up. Some fell on rocky places, where it did not have much soil. It sprang up quickly, because the soil was shallow. But when the sun came up, the plants were scorched, and they withered because they had no root. Other seed fell among thorns, which grew up and choked the plants. Still other seeds fell on good soil, where it produced a crop—a hundred, sixty or thirty times what was sown. Whoever has ears, let them hear."

Hosea 10:12
Sow righteousness for yourselves, reap the fruit of unfailing love, and break up your unplowed ground; for it is time to seek the LORD, until he comes and showers his righteousness on you.

*　　*　　*

It starts with the earth. We humans are of the earth. In fact, the word "human" is derived from the Latin, *humus*, which means earth. From the very beginning, we are inextricably connected to the soil. So, it makes sense that we are drawn to the garden to sustain us physically and spiritually. It is home. We figuratively came from it and likewise, will return to it (ashes to ashes, dust to dust).

We continue to use humus as a scientific term to describe the top layer of the decomposing organic elements that builds up over time. It is the rich, black, fertile soil that plants love. It's the good stuff. Soil also takes on various forms depending on the type and texture of weathered rock it is comprised of. We can describe the earth beneath our feet as sand, silt or clay. Each has its good and bad points.

Too much or too little of any of these can have an impact on the foundational soil of a garden making gardening difficult, if not impossible. The ideal garden bed base, called "loam," is a mixture of 40% sand, 40% silt, and 20% clay. The soil needs to balance its ability to hold water, air and nutrients. Christ's parable of the seed sower provides a way to consider each one of these essential elements in a little more detail and how it all connects to our spirituality.

Sand is very familiar, as we've played in it and with it at the beach or playgrounds. It is so porous that it sifts through our fingers. Sand is fluid and malleable, allowing it to shift and move. And with the right amount of moisture, we can shape sand into a form, like a sandcastle. While sand can stand and take shape, it is not very sturdy, and eventually, it will collapse. Like sand, we've played around with clay at one time or another in our life. Again, depending on how much moisture or heat is added, we can shape clay into something. But unlike sand, the form we shape clay into can actually harden and hold its shape. The down side of hardened clay is that once it achieves this state, it has no flexibility and can only break when pressure is exerted on it. Silt, on the other hand, is a little less familiar to us. Like sand and clay, silt is made of weathered rock but it is much lighter in texture making it more like dust. Because of this, silt is very movable and easily transported in the air (as in dust storms) and water. We are familiar with this characteristic when we learn about river delta areas that grow in mass due to silt being deposited by the river water. But too much silt actually creates mud, such as the mud that accumulates in and around structures during flooding. And like our playful experience with sand and clay, we know that mud can be molded into shape like mud pies, but it can be very difficult to work with when there's too much silt. As a result, it becomes mucky and sticky rendering it next to impossible to work with.

The foundation of our spirituality (and personality for that matter) is based on the same type of characteristics found in the elements of soil. Too much or too little of a particular aspect makes it difficult to shape, form, and work with. We need to have the right balance of each of these elements for our spiritual foundation. Our spirituality requires some flexibility and fluidity. Similarly, we need the strength and hardness of clay to be firm and stand. Finally, we need some lightness that allows movement. But, like our own childlike and playful experiences with sand, clay, and mud, we recognize that each of these elements has their limitations. If we are too loose in our spiritual lives, nothing will take root and grow. If we are too hard and firm, nothing will take root and grow and we run the risk of breaking. If we are too mucked up and sticky, nothing will take root and grow. Deep down inside, each of us knows that our spirituality foundation may be out of balance, just as Christ illustrated in His parable.

So, to have a garden, we need a patch of dirt. It can't be just any old dirt, as we have seen. It has to have all this good stuff in it. What we hope to produce must literally be grounded because we plant seeds in the ground. It is incumbent upon the gardener to have a solid, healthy foundation for growth to occur. The same is true of our spirituality. In addition to the essential elements of sand, clay, and silt, the soil requires nutrients. As mentioned above, humus is comprised of organic compounds, and is alive with billions of microorganisms. It is the quality and quantity of these elements that make the soil healthy. The healthier the soil, the healthier the crops that come from it. Similarly, the healthier our *soul*, (composed of quality "compounds,") the healthier our spiritual lives will be. So it helps to take stock of our spiritual foundation. We take soil samples to see what our dirt has and lacks. Based upon the results of that investigation, we know what to add or minimize. Fertilizers add nitrogen, phosphorus, and potassium as well as secondary elements of calcium, sulfur and magnesium. Other additives help balance pH, and increase tilth, which is the ability to work the soil. Think of all of this as vitamins for the soil.

Like the soil, our soul and spirituality need some spiritual vitamins for spiritual nourishment. This whole book is designed to provide spiritual nourishment. Some basic spiritual vitamins you can add to and strengthen your spiritual foundation are briefly listed here and explored in more detail throughout this book. These include using guided reading and reflection materials, journaling, resting in the Sabbath, pilgrimage, fasting from food or certain forms of technology, retreating into solitude, and joining in fellowship with others through sharing a meal or book discussion.

Our spiritual life is also grounded in values and beliefs that enrich the foundation of our life. We must be aware of and understand that foundation. The word "understand" means we stand on the principles and knowledge that hold us up. We are "grounded" on the beliefs on which we stand. However, these valued beliefs are not always integrated into our everyday lives as something to ground us and act upon. Instead, they are relegated to abstract and noble principles to hold in theory. The gardener may "know" and "believe" that weeding and watering are important for crops to grow. But that knowledge and belief alone are not enough, as the plants will not grow on their own without the gardener actually applying that knowledge and belief. It is very easy to say one believes in all of these values. The challenge is living them out everyday and not just for a few hours on a Sunday morning. These values become our spiritual foundation from which our spiritual growth stems. What it all comes down to is not what we consider important or what we think to be true but rather, it is how we live out those values and beliefs. Otherwise, we are standing upon quicksand rather than firm, solid ground.

Soil that has been disturbed by heavy equipment, such as at a building site or along roads, becomes the breeding ground for a whole host of pesky growth that is hard to control and runs the risk of taking over. The traumatized earth has been stripped away of its healthy topsoil and what is left is compacted and squashed. Invasive types of plants such as thorns, thistles and weeds can easily colonize the disturbed ground because they don't require rich fertile soil, allowing them to readily invade and take root in this disturbed and weakened dirt. Nature doesn't want any gaps or spaces! So it starts filling in blank spots, often with these unwanted and opportunistic types of plants that don't require the same type of healthy base. On top of that, these pesky plants can easily spread and take over. It is difficult, if not impossible, for a fruitful garden to come to life when soil has been stripped of the top layer of nutrients and then compacted. Metaphorically, the same can be true of our own traumatized and compacted spirituality.

Whims and fads, pundits on TV, economic worries, and corrupt politics can all strip away and compact our own spiritual foundation. Busy hectic schedules can squash the life out of us. When this happens, we, too, are at risk of having pesky opportunistic weeds and thorns take root in our own spirituality and take over our lives. In our weakened state, we are vulnerable to fears, bad habits, and a lifestyle that drains the life out of us. We try to fill in the space with a weedy lifestyle of accumulated stuff or behaviors that can quickly take over our lives. Like a gardener, we need to again build the soft, fertile soil that we can stand upon, supporting the good work and life that is intended by God through our relationships, study, discipleship, prayer, worship and thought.

The process of taking a "soul sample" reflects one of the opening quotes to this passage, as it may be very revealing. But the mere act of gardening—of what we do or don't do—to harvest our crops may also reveal something of our spirituality.

Reflection

What type of soil describes your current spiritual foundation? Refer to the parable in Matthew that describes the ability of the Word to take root in your life.

Is your personal and spiritual foundation so hard that the seeds get eaten before they can take root?

Is your spiritual topsoil so thin and deficient that although the Word may sprout, there is nothing in it to sustain it when the troubling times of drought and sunburn come?

Has your foundation been disturbed to the point that only distractions take root? Is your life so full of distractions (thorns and weeds) that there is no room for the Word to flourish in your life?

Or have you attended to the health of your spiritual soil, so that it can support lush and fruitful growth?

What can you do to build up your foundation? How can you make your soul alive and well, so it can support the purpose that God has in mind for you?

Tips for Cultivating your Spirituality

Study! Join a Bible study group, read inspirational books and delve deeper into the history and literature of the most bought and least read book on the planet: the Bible.

Go on a Media diet—reject the pundits, fear mongers, extremists and the dividers that permeate the media.

Refuse to listen to only one side, but balance one argument with a counter argument so that you can see all sides of an issue.

Start a gratitude journal, count your blessings, and give thanks for all the goodness in your life. By focusing on what you have, rather than what you don't, you can start to build up by adding more and more good things to your life.

Give back. The soil must be replenished with compost, humus, fertilizer, in order to continue supporting good works. Give yourself time for replenishment by resting or observing the Sabbath (see Chapter 4 on fallow land below), and put good things back into your soil through study, right relationships, good thoughts, and Paul's list of fruit of the spirit: love, joy, peace, patience, kindness, generosity, faithfulness, gentleness, and self control (see chapter on compost).

Prayer

Gracious God—

You are the foundation of our lives. We promise to cultivate the gifts and blessings you have provided.

Amen.

Chapter 2

Faith: Seeds and Planting

Seedling for Thought

Nourish beginnings, let us nourish beginnings. Not all things are blest, but the seeds of all things are blest. The blessing is in the seed.

~ Muriel Rukeyser

Scripture

Matthew 17:20
He replied, "Because you have so little faith. Truly I tell you, if you have faith as small as a mustard seed, you can say to this mountain, 'Move from here to there,' and it will move. Nothing will be impossible for you."

*   *   *

Planting seeds in a garden is an act of faith. We place a little, tiny button of life into a hole in the ground trusting it will grow. Now keep in mind we don't place the entire responsibility of growth on the seed. We have a role in the process. We have to water it and tend to the seedling as it starts to grow. In some ways, this act of faith goes both ways. The seed has as much faith in the gardener as the gardener has in planting the seed.

Most of us experience faith to some extent in our everyday life. We have faith in the cook who prepares our meal, in the engineer who designed the bridge we drive over, in the surgeon who is about to operate on us. To some extent, these are examples of "blind faith" as we don't even "see" or bother thinking about the ramifications of not having faith in these examples. If we did think about it too much, we would paralyze ourselves with fear and could not function or get through life. The word "faith" itself comes from the Latin, root of *fidere* "to trust." When we trust, we have confidence and perhaps even a sense of courage. When this is the case, we overcome our fear. Faith is trust—in our self and in others. It means having confidence in the gifts and talents God has given us. When we think of faith in this way, we come to realize that we are, in some respects, like the seed. Only in this case, God is the gardener who has faith in us—waiting and watching for us to sprout and grow.

Seeds are the beginnings of something to come. As we hold these small, seemingly insignificant flecks in our hand, it is almost impossible to imagine they will grow into something as big and wonderful as a crop that will sustain us. Outside the garden, it is mind-boggling to regard a mighty oak as starting from a single acorn. Much of what we do in our lives is the same process. An idea starts small, and with time and attention it grows into something much bigger that sustains us. In a literal sense, we were all seedlings. Parents, families, and friends waited for our arrival in the world and then watched us grow.

And, while a certain amount of care, such as watering, is required, we simply wait. We wait and watch for the seedling to poke its head out of the soil. We experience a sense of anticipation of something to come. Waiting also provides us an opportunity to wonder. By sitting and perhaps staring at the dirt, we allow our thoughts and imagination to take seed and sprout. We might suddenly marvel at the sheer wonder of the gardening process. In this way, we reconnect with the earth and the mystery of the earth. The act of waiting is an opportunity to contemplate—to simply rest our bodies and let our minds do what it does best—to think and ponder. This is exactly what Mary and the world experience during the season of Advent. The waiting and anticipation that is Advent gives us an opportunity in a crazy, busy world to marvel, ponder, and wonder at the possibilities of what is to come. *This is when God finds us.* This aptly describes what we are called to do in Psalm 46—"Be still and know that I am God." To what extent, if at all, do we find the time in our busy lives to wait, watch, and wonder, allowing God to find us? For many, it just doesn't happen and we don't give ourselves permission—we forget that we've been invited to do just that—"be still."

But, as good as this waiting business can be, it is also tough to handle, especially in this day and age of instant information and instant gratification. We have grown accustomed to getting anything and everything we want and need—from finding the factoid of the population of a city to "fast food" in a drive-through window. That's part of the problem—we've forgotten how to wait. Waiting, as much as we may not want to admit, is a part of life. We become impatient or frustrated when life does not move as quickly as we'd like it to move. This has even crept into the modest "agricultural" aspects of contemporary suburban life when an entire front yard can quite literally be rolled out in sections of pre-fabricated strips of sod. Voila! Instant lawn. We can't even wait for seasonal food, leading us to forget (or never realize) that certain produce grow at certain times of the year. There was a time when we used to wait and eagerly anticipate when amazing tomatoes or certain fruits would ripen and be available to enjoy. Now, we have "hot houses" where we trick Mother Nature into growing things out of season, or we ship that produce from other parts of the world where it is in season. In reality, gardens (and life) don't work that way. Waiting is part of the deal, like it or not. We can also remind ourselves that waiting can be fun. As children we eagerly anticipated birthdays and holidays.

But waiting does not mean we're not doing anything. The garden offers plenty of other matters to tend to while we wait. In fact, paying attention to those other things will help us tend to the seedlings that will eventually turn into fully-grown crops. We can be gathering mulch that will be spread later. We can be sharpening tools, turning compost, and weeding garden paths. We can also be reading and studying about gardening. This is cultivating a setting that nurtures growth to come.

In a sense, this waiting and preparation creates opportunities for growth. Think about the waiting process of expecting a baby's arrival. We don't sit and wait—we prepare our lives for this new adventure. We fix up the nursery, we get baby clothes, we get a crib, we start saving money for college, and we read books and talk to others about what to do. The same is true in our own lives. We can create opportunities for ourselves to grow by sharpening our own mental and spiritual tools through networking with others, studying, looking for similar experiences or people who share our interests.

Life, like gardening, is a process that requires attention, effort, and . . . yes, waiting. But the waiting is not the same kind as what occurs when we sit down at a restaurant "waiting" for a "waiter" to serve us and bring us something. Over time, our sense of waiting has evolved into this mentality of entitlement as we wait and watch for an end to war or poverty. We wait and watch for a clean and healthy environment. We wait and watch for good health to suddenly appear out of nowhere. We hold this expectation, or perhaps even a sense of entitlement, that all of these things will simply "pop up" on their own or that some one else will take care of this—maybe even God. Most of us have, at one time or another prayed or wondered why God allows things like war or poverty to happen. And God is wondering why WE allowed these things to happen by us or by anyone. We have forgotten that a single seed for each of these things must be planted. We can plant the seeds of destruction and hate or we can plant the seeds of prosperity and peace in the geo-political garden as well as the garden of our personal lives. It's really up to us. And even when that seed has been planted, we have the role and responsibility of tending to its growth. We are the gardeners of peace, prosperity, a clean environment, and good health. We are the ones to plant the seeds. We must ask ourselves how are we tending to these things as we would tend to seedlings in the garden—or are we?

We can start with the little things in our lives. We can change the way we behave to promote harmony between people we interact with or nurture a healthy environment and a healthy self. Others will see these efforts. This is what Christ meant in Matthew 5:14 when he said, "YOU are the light of the world." Others must see evidence of YOU "being" a certain way so they can have faith in you. Your life partner, children, and closest friends have faith in you—not because there is a set of rules written down somewhere telling them they are "supposed" to have faith in you—but because of the way you tend to them (just as we tend the garden) and act in general. In this context, it is easier to see how faith is more about trust than it is in believing in written rules or dogma. This is what Christ did. He modeled for us the way we should "be" with others. This is why we try to live a Christ-like life and "be a light." Christ lived his life in a way that is easy to be faith-full so we have trust and confidence in him. So we must ask ourselves to what extent we live a Christ-like life so that others can have "faith" in us? How do we go about acting out in the way we live our life in such a way that others can have *faith in us*? How are we faithful to our marriage, family, and our own well-being?

Beyond our amazement that a crop will evolve out of this unassuming seed is the equally amazing fact that every crop generates its own seed to help propagate more of the same in the future. Every fruit and vegetable leaves behind a seed to be re-planted. In a sense, each and every plant leaves behind a legacy. Christ speaks of this in John 12:24, *"Very truly I tell you, unless a kernel of wheat falls to the ground and dies, it remains only a single seed. But if it dies, it produces many seeds."* There is a lovely irony to this. What is the seed or legacy we leave behind? What is it about your own life and life's accomplishment that you are leaving behind for others to use in their own growth?

So faith is all about trust and waiting—just as we plant seeds in the garden. We close this passage by referring to the opening passage of this book to be reminded that "everything" started off in the garden and in a sense, God was and is the ultimate gardener. If that is the case, we can take comfort in knowing that our own personal and spiritual sprouting is an act of faith on God's part. He has faith in <u>us.</u> We tend to get caught up in and focused on it being the other way around when it's really a two-way process. If God can have faith in us, why can't we have faith in our self?

Reflection

What does "faith" mean or look like to you? What are some "everyday" examples or acts of faith in your life?

Have you ever contemplated the fact that God has faith in you?

What is a skill/talent/interest you had early on in your life that you've nurtured or developed? How and why did you "tend" to this? What was the outcome?

What is it about you and the way you live your life that others can and do have faith in you?

How and when (if at all) do you take time to "be still?" Why or why not?

What are some examples of impatience in your own life? What are some ways you can have faith and create opportunities for growth?

What seeds have you planted that will be your legacy? What do you hope your legacy will be?

Tips for Cultivating Your Spirituality

Take and make time to sit and be still. You have permission to do so and it's not a waste of time. That is where God is waiting to find you.

Create opportunities for your own personal and spiritual growth by reading, journaling, and sharing with others.

Consider ways you can plant the seed of peace and prosperity in your own life. What aspect of you needs tending to?

Intentionally consider your legacy. What can you leave behind that will help and serve others? Be sure everything is in place for your legacy to be harvested.

Think of one interest or skill you'd like to develop. Go to the library, get online, talk to others to learn ways you can nurture this seedling in your own life.

Prayer

Gracious God—
Thank you for the seeds you've given me. It is up to me to plant and care for them. I will tend to them just as you tend to me. May my life be a legacy and testament to you and others so that they may grow and prosper.

Amen.

Chapter 3

Weeds: Spiritual Discernment

Seedlings for Thought

You must weed your mind as you would weed your garden.

~ Astrid Alauda

They know, they just know where to grow, how to dupe you, and how to camouflage themselves among the perfectly respectable plants, they just know, and therefore, I've concluded weeds must have brains.

~ Dianne Benson

For me the appropriate metaphor for the inner spiritual center is a garden, a place of potential peace and tranquility. This garden is a place where the Spirit of God comes to make self-disclosure to share wisdom, to give affirmation or rebuke, to provide encouragement, and to give direction and guidance. When this garden is in proper order, it is a quiet place, and there is an absence of busyness, of defiling noise, of confusion. The inner garden is a delicate place, and if not properly maintained it will be quickly overrun by intrusive under-growth. God does not often walk in disordered gardens. And that is why inner gardens that are ignored are said to be empty.

~ Gordon MacDonald

Scripture

Matthew 13:22 (New International Version)
The one who received the seed that fell among the thorns is the person who hears the word, but the worries of this life and the deceitfulness of wealth chokes the word, making it unfruitful.

*　　*　　*

The California Master Gardner handbook defines a weed as:

Any plant growing out of place; a plant growing where it is unwanted or interferes with more desirous plants.

Why don't we want weeds? Because they steal the nutrients from the good plants or they can overtake and choke the plants. In short, weeds just get in the way of growth. Curiously, there are also a lot of "good plants" that can spring up in the wrong place. Despite their usefulness in providing nutrition or beauty, they too, can choke out our immediate needs and demand our immediate attention, sucking our time and energy away from something else that might be more important or productive.

Our only recourse is to weed out those pesky things that take root and grow where we don't want or need them. And while we recognize the importance and need, let's face it: weeding is one of the least attractive and unromantic aspects of gardening. Poems are not written about weeding. It is a perfunctory task. It probably takes more time than planting, watering, and direct care of the plants we love. And yet, without attending to weeds, they can overtake and choke out what grows. Weeding requires attention and noticing. It demands that we recognize the difference between a seedling and a weed. Inexperienced gardeners are prone to accidentally pull up a sprout instead of a weed. It is a process of agricultural discernment. Weeding requires effort. A tired or careless gardener runs the same risk by becoming distracted. What does one pay attention to?

Is weeding boring or can it be a form of prayer where we can get lost in our thoughts? Some characterize the task as being very "Zen" which can be thought of in Christian context as meditation or prayer. We can escape momentarily from the world focusing instead on the task and the weeds within ourselves. We can also re-focus ourselves to weed out the sins and shortcomings of our own life. Helena Rutherford Ely wrote in, *A Woman's*

Hardy Garden, "I always think of my sins when I weed. They grow apace in the same way and are harder still to get rid of."

When weeding, it is important to get to the root and pull it out or it will only re-emerge later on. That takes effort. Quick-fix chemical sprays are convenient, but they run the risk of killing other things along with the weeds.

Bindweed is the bane of many gardeners. Some would swear it seems like there is only one giant common root that sends off countless runners throughout the earth's surface because it just doesn't seem possible to ever get rid of it. As pesky as it seems, bindweed is actually nature's way of sustaining moisture. Its deep roots actually lift moisture from the depths of the earth to the topsoil. Likewise, bindweed can serve as a kind of living mulch that shades the next layer of vegetation and creates favorable conditions for growing. Despite all these seemingly useful attributes, bindweed is prolific and can take over a garden thus becoming a weed by definition. Our challenge in discernment or spiritual weeding is determining if the "weeds" in our daily spiritual life actually serve a purpose or are they overtaking our "spiritual garden" demanding time and effort for maintenance.

Reflection

What are the weeds in your life? What crops up out of nowhere, demanding your time, attention, and energy that is taken away from nurturing the rest of your life?

How and when do you choose to "weed" in our life? How do you determine or discern the difference between a weed and a useful plant?

What are the cares and worries of the world that chokes your spiritual growth in life's garden?

Tips for Cultivating Your Spirituality

Take a look at how you spend your time. Break a typical day into 30-minute blocks of time and list what you do. Discern if this is how you truly wish to spend your time. If not, what can you "weed out" from your life or daily routine?

Take a look at how you spend your money. Examine your monthly bills and checkbook. Are you a good steward of your money? If not, what expenses might you "weed out" of your spending?

Take time to notice where you find joy and God's presence in your life. Cultivate those things. Take time to notice where you don't find joy or God. Consider steps or actions you might take to keep those moments and situations from overtaking your life.

Take time to notice and determine where the weeds seem to "pop up" and thrive. Are there good aspects of your life that are like good plants but seem to over run or overtake your life?

We quipped earlier that no one writes poetry about weeding. Yet the Psalms often included laments about life's challenges, which could be characterized as weeds. Consider writing your own Psalm or poem about your life's "weeds" as a form of prayer and lamentation to God. By naming the "weeds" in ones life, we ask for God's help for yanking them up and out of life's garden.

Prayer:

Gracious God—

We know that we often allow weeds to pop up in our lives. We know these weeds zap what sustains us and chokes us. Help and guide us to get to the root of all those unwanted things that invade our lives and weed them out.

Amen

Chapter 4

Fallow Land: Sabbath and Rest

Seedlings for Thought

Gardening is about enjoying the smell of things growing in the soil, getting dirty without feeling guilty, and generally taking the time to soak up a little peace and serenity.

~ Lindley Karstens

Scripture

Leviticus 25:3-5
For six years sow your fields, and for six years prune your vineyards and gather their crops. But in the seventh year the land is to have a year of Sabbath rest, a Sabbath to the Lord. Do not sow your fields or prune your vineyards. Do not reap what grows of itself or harvest the grapes of your untended vines. The land is to have a year of rest.

*   *   *

Garden soil works very hard to give us produce. It uses up important chemicals and nutrients in the process. And while we don't tend to think of soil in this way, this plot of land it is actually a living thing. All living things require sustenance and rest. The soil in the garden requires both so we allow it lie fallow or un-used for a period of time. Fallow is essentially an agricultural form of Sabbath. We give the soil a rest to recover from chemical and nutrient depletion that occurs through growing produce. As the opening scripture says, the practice of fallow fields has been known for ages. Likewise, recent American history demonstrates what happens when we ignore this fact of nature. The "dust bowl" of the late 1920s was largely a result of over-working the land, reducing it to almost nothing and rendering it useless so it blew away. That image aptly describes the lives of many of us. We work so hard that we become worn down to the point that any major stressor in life that comes along "blows us away" emotionally and physically.

Attentive gardeners realize the importance of letting the soil rest in order to revitalize it. Ideally, specific plots are set aside each year to rest for a year without planting any garden produce. But total non-use of plots may not be feasible, so if nothing else, use a cover crop or another way of sustaining the land, like applying manure or compost when the garden is put to bed for the winter. A cover crop, sometimes known as "green manure," also restores nutrients in the soil. Cover crops might include legumes such as fava beans, bell beans, and vetch. All in all, the garden has earned a well-deserved break or Sabbath.

Gardeners have known and practiced allowing the soil to rest for eons. Unfortunately, we don't always apply the same principle or practice to our own lives. We don't allow our own lives to lay fallow or to have a Sabbath.

When we hear the word Sabbath, many of us associate it with a specific day, which in Christian tradition is Sunday. But the Sabbath can be a practice carried out any time and anywhere. Wayne Mueller has written a great book on the Sabbath, called . . . well—*Sabbath: Finding Rest, Renewal, and Delight In Our Busy Lives.* In it, he reminds us that Sabbath is not just the absence of work or having a day off. Instead, it is when we dedicate time and attention to notice the presence of a certain kind of feeling or spirit that nourishes us. The idea and practice of Sabbath is a very real aspect of our spirituality. It isn't tied up in complicated rituals or dogma. It is merely resting in the presence of God. To be Christ-like is to rest—just as he did. It is not a luxury—it is a gift. In Mark 2: 27 Christ taught that the Sabbath was made for humans and not the other way around. It is not a waste of time—it is a saving or investment of time that will pay off in dividends in other parts of our crazy lives. Keep in mind, even God rested after creating the world and if the Almighty needed to hit the pause button, so can you. You might be asking yourself: if God and Christ were both able to practice Sabbath, why is it so hard for me to do the same?

Our culture is constantly sending and reinforcing the message of "doing." We are perpetually in motion and busy, equating all this doing as being productive. Yes, our rushing about and multi-tasking certainly does produce many outcomes, including fatigue. Many of us feel that our lives are out of control. Every minute of the day is jammed. We are running around frantically trying to accomplish this and that, with little or no room in our life for another single thing. We feel like we can barely breath and that we have to catch our breath. And let's face it—suffocation is not particularly good for you. "Catching our breath" is a spiritual act as it allows us to sustain ourselves while connecting to and with others.

A number of things happen when we rest. From a physical standpoint, our tired bodies have a chance to re-charge. Even when we work out in a gym, we have to stop to catch our breath and allow our muscles time to recover from the stress. Otherwise, our bodies would shut down and we would collapse on to the gym floor. Rest is good from a psychological standpoint as well. All of us have uttered the expression, "I couldn't think straight because I was so tired." That is not merely a euphemism; it is an accurate description of our inability to cognitively process what's going on when we are tired. We make poor decisions when our brain is cluttered and overworked. Socially, taking time off from our busy-ness provides time to "be" with an-other—like family and friends. We are social animals and interacting with an-other, especially those we love, feeds their soul as well as ours. Conversely, resting also provides us an opportunity for solitude, which is perhaps the more important (and ironically least understood or valued) spiritual benefit of rest. It allows us to be in the presence of God. It is an opportunity to hang out with God. And when that happens, we begin to notice and hear His voice speak to us.

We need to remember that in Luke 5:15-16 Christ knew when it was time to take a break and went off into the wilderness to get away from it all. He even advised his disciples to do the same in Mark 6:31. If Christ and the disciples can do it—we can too. We need to intentionally make space in our lives to rest and rejuvenate our bodies and spirit. Space can be a physical or mental location that can be occupied or vacated. It is up to us as to what fills that space or how we use it. The garden may be one physical space where you can shut down from the usual day-to-day rush and just tinker.

Despite being a physical activity, talking a walk or riding a bike may also actually be a form of rest, especially mental rest, though they involve an element of physical "doing." Sitting alone in the low light of the morning eating a bowl of cereal, taking that evening walk, listening to music, or pulling weeds in the garden are all forms of resting that do not involve a lot of effort. We can think of these activities as a spiritual "cover crop" that restores our soul. Of course, we've been socialized to view them as a "waste of time," as we are not "accomplishing" anything. In reality, we have carved out time for ourselves and for God and allowed a small part of our busy lives to lie fallow. Think of Sabbath as hanging out and spending time with God. It is also a chance to get re-acquainted with our self. Give yourself permission. After all, Christ does.

Reflection

Where and when do you practice the Sabbath—or do you practice Sabbath?

Where is a place you have been or go to where you feel absolute bliss? What is it about this place that is so blissful? Are there ways you can incorporate some of the elements into your life without actually going there?

What are some examples in which you are engaged in some sort of mindless activity that might be a "cover crop" that is actually restorative and regenerating to you?

Where and how might you carve out time and space just for you? Talk about this with your family so they understand why you're doing this.

Take a look at your calendar. What is it telling you?

Are you checking e-mails from work over the weekend?

Tips For Cultivating Your Spirituality

Try "e-fasting" on Sunday, avoiding any communication associated with your job.

Identify a nearby place that is special and feeds your soul. Go there and "do nothing" at least once a week.

Intentionally mark out some time in your daily calendar to take a walk or find a place at your workplace where you can "take a break" without others around.

Consider attending a "different" worship service for a change.

Consider going to a different denominational worship service once in a while.

Prayer

Gracious God—
Give me permission to rest. Remind me that it is OK to take a time out. Let me find the time and space to catch my breath so I might be stronger and grow.

Amen

Chapter 5

Lean On Me: Staking and Spacing

Seedlings for Thought

A garden is so much like a church. So much care and feeding. Such competitiveness among the plants—some of them literally choke each other to death if you don't get out there and put a stop to it. The big gorgeous ones get lots of attention, but then one comes along that looks almost dead all season and suddenly, almost overnight, blooms splendidly forth. Never write anybody off completely. You just don't know.

~ Barbara Cawthorne Crafton

Scripture

Judges 16: 26
Samson said to the servant who held his hand, "Put me where I can feel the pillars that support the temple, so that I may lean against them."

*   *   *

Certain types of plants in the garden, like tomatoes, need to be held up because they grow too big and tall to stand on their own. Without proper support, their branches rest on the ground and run the risk of rotting or becoming infested by pests, such as worms or snails, that suck the life out of the plant. So we provide stakes, trellises, or cages. This is a proactive process of knowing and anticipating the need for support. The gardener intentionally installs the support mechanism of staking. It doesn't just happen—stakes do not magically appear. Like the gardener, we must acknowledge the need for spiritual support and intentionally identify and install the staking that will support our spiritual growth.

It is a bit ironic that something so big and strong like a tomato plant requires that kind of support whereas something as un-assuming as the eggplant can grow just fine on its own. Even the strong and powerful Samson sought the physical and spiritual support of the temple to lean on. His muscular power by itself was not adequate. Many of us have internal fortitude and confidence that provide inner strength. But even then, we thrive with adequate support. The same is true for our spiritual growth. On the other hand, there are individuals who struggle with their inner strength and spirituality. They, too, need some staking to support their spiritual growth. The type of spiritual staking can vary—there is no one way to support one's spiritual growth. Many individuals bear a tremendous weight from life's demands. In those moments when we are without adequate support, we run the risk of falling over, or becoming "infested" with pests that can drain the life from us. In moments of weakness, we may begin to search for and rely on other less healthy devices that *seem* to provide the support we need—devices such as alcohol, drugs, gambling, sex, or work.

Peter A. Campbell and Edwin M. McMahon are Christian psychologists who characterize addiction as substituting one feeling, behavior, or attitude for another, rather than addressing the real problem or situation. Healthier forms of support include a life partner, family member, good friend, or a community of faith. As discussed in the introduction of this book, spirituality is really about relationships—with others, God's creation, God, and our self. These relationships are the pillars we can lean on. And like the practice of staking in gardening, tending to our own spiritual growth can include practices that nurture our spirituality and relationships. Taking a walk, reading scripture or inspirational writings, prayer, writing in journals, doing volunteer service—even working in a garden—can provide the spiritual staking and sacred space we need to support and tend to our own spiritual needs.

In addition to the physical support of staking that some plants need to thrive, *all* plants require adequate space to grow. If they are too crowded, they will compete with each other to derive the nutrients they need from the soil, and suffocate from lack of adequate air and sunlight. The prudent gardener approaches this problem in a couple of ways. Early on in planning and planting the garden, seeds, or seedlings are placed in the soil with sufficient space between them. Later, as the plants begin to grow, the gardener will "thin" plants by pulling out ones that are too close together. Selecting what should stay and what should go allows healthy growth. Gardeners will "prune" or cut plants back so they can grow and thrive. We are the same way. While we are social beings requiring the company and fellowship of others, we must have adequate space for ourselves that allows us to grow spiritually as well. When we carve out a few moments from our hectic lives, we allow ourselves the opportunity to draw upon the spiritual nutrients that nurture our *soul* and spirit in the same way a plant in the garden draws upon the nutrients in the *soil* through its roots.

But that nurturing process is threatened or compromised when those roots are tangled up with other plants competing for the same nutrients. Our busy lives and calendars compete for the same attention and sustenance as our spirits. It is impossible to nurture our spirituality—relationships with ourselves, others, creation, and God—when we are running around doing a million things. There is no "space" in the day to tend to our spiritual needs when our day planner is full or over-flowing. Consequently, we realize we may need to "thin out" our daily lives by pulling out the activities that are choking off our survival and healthy growth. In our culture, we tend to view busyness and productivity as good—and it is—but NOT to the point it chokes our own personal health and growth.

We are socialized to think that every waking moment in our lives must be full of doing. That is not the same thing as "being." In the long run, we fool ourselves into thinking that creating space to tend to and nurture our own spirituality and relationships is either "selfish" or a "waste of time" because it does not meet our cultural expectation of full and crowded living. It doesn't work in the garden, so why should we think it would work in our personal and spiritual lives?

Conversely, this frenetic busyness can sometimes become a coping mechanism that serves as a distraction from deeper needs or issues. When we do make sacred space, we may have to pay attention to what bubbles up within us, and that can be scary. Our busyness becomes one of the devices we use as a substitute for one feeling, behavior, or attitude over another, conveniently distracting us from nurturing our spirituality and relationship with God. For many, it is "easier" to be busy than to listen to the conversation that might occur if we carve out time to listen to what God has to say to us. And, just as the gardener tends to the garden, God is tending to us. It is a process that provides growth and yields a harvest of a fulfilling life. We can "lean" on God as well as kindred spirits. Through our relationships with God, our life partner, family, friends and community of faith, we are provided the staking and spacing that allows us to grow.

Reflection

What and/or who are the "stakes" that supports you? Have you proactively "installed" those stakes to anticipate the things that might "knock you over?" If so, how do they provide the spiritual support you need? If not, how might you go about installing the stakes you need?

What "nutrients" in your life sustain you?

What might be getting tangled up in your own spiritual roots that reduce your ability to draw upon the nutrients of life that sustain you?

Are there any "spiritual pests" that "eat away" at your spiritual and/or personal life when you "fall over" from the weight of everything? What kind of "spiritual pest management" might you utilize to ward these "pests" away?

Take a look at your weekly calendar. What does it say to you? Is there space that allows you to nurture and tend to your spirituality and relationship with your self, others, God's creation, and God? If not, when, where, and how might you provide the space you need to tend to your own spiritual garden?

Finally, how might you be a support for another person in your life garden? Do you know people who could use your help and strength to lean on during tough times?

Tips for Cultivating Your Spirituality

Send a note of thanks to someone you lean on—let them know you need them and appreciate them.

Look for books, films, or music that can help sustain you during tough times.

Look at your calendar and determine what the "pests" are in your life. Think of ways you can either manage them or get rid of them altogether. Talk with those you trust and support you for their opinion and feedback.

Think of a family member or friend who has come to lean on you. Ponder the ways you support them and think about possible new ways that might excite or revitalize both of you.

Prayer

Gracious God—

I know I can lean on you. Thank you for family and friends who support me. Give me the strength to support them in their difficult times.

Amen.

Chapter 6

Spiritual Photosynthesis: Sunlight, Water, and Air

Seedling for Thought:

There's nothing more spiritual than watching what you've planted in the ground. You plant it, you nurture it, and God provides the sun and the rain and helps it to grow. You see the absolute mystery in what God has given to us in growing things . . . also the absolute beauty. There's beauty in the simplest of things — the flowers or the bark of a tree. Sometimes it behooves us to stop and look.

~ Sister Christine

Scripture:

Job 8:16
They are like a well-watered plant in the sunshine, spreading its shoots over the garden.

*   *   *

Gardens are solar-powered food factories. The leaf structures on plants are essentially solar panels, collecting sunlight. However, plants convert light into chemical energy while solar panels convert light into electric energy. Both collect sunlight that stimulates electrons to create energy or fuel. Plants have proteins containing chlorophylls (that's what make them green) that use the solar energy to split water molecules to create carbon dioxide that helps the plant "breathe" and produce sugar (fuel). This generates and releases oxygen as a by-product, which we breathe.

A key element within the process is water, which plants suck up from earth through their roots, much like a straw. Contained in that water are nutrients from the soil that support the production of sugar as fuel that basically "feeds" the plant. Water is also partially accumulated through the leaves. Each plant has its own internal plumbing system to circulate the water. Contained in that water are nutrients from the soil that support the production of sugar as fuel that basically "feeds" the plant. This is a water-based circulatory system, much like our own blood circulatory system.

A plant needs both sunlight and water to grow. Energy is collected so that one set of chemicals is transformed or changed into another set of chemicals as fuel that sustains the plant. This process is called photosynthesis. It is a complex symbiotic cycle that both plants and humans rely on. That's it for the science lesson.

The gardener knows the basics here—a garden needs sunlight, water, and air to sustain it. Think of this as sort of an agricultural trinity consisting of three separate elements that combine in a single process. Without appropriate amounts of all three, chemical interaction and transformation cannot take place and the plants basically shut down. Therefore, a gardener must choose a garden site with adequate sunlight. An astute gardener knows where and how to arrange garden crops so taller plants don't block the sunlight from the smaller ones. Likewise, the climatic conditions of the area must provide enough rain. If that's not the case, the gardener has to intervene and help out by providing the water.

Our spirituality is much like the garden in this respect. It too, requires essential elements that go through a transformation process to sustain it. This can be illustrated with a little exercise. Sitting right here and now, take a breath and hold it. You don't need to take a huge, gulp of air as if you were blowing out birthday candles or getting ready to dive into a swimming pool—just take a breath and hold it. Do it now.

*   *   *

Welcome back. Now, just take another minute or so to jot down or take mental inventory of what you noticed or experienced during those few seconds of holding your breath.

*   *   *

This exercise has been conducted a number of times in various settings. In a group situation, it is possible to discuss the discoveries that come from the exercise. Over the years, typical responses include statements such as, "*I became aware of sounds in the room that I hadn't noticed before*," or "*I felt my body relax a bit*," and conversely others have reported, "*I felt myself tense up because I was so focused on holding my breath*." Still, others have shared, "*I became aware of my thoughts and how my mind wandered*," or "*I suddenly became aware of others in the room*." Finally, one brave and often somewhat reluctant individual eventually states the embarrassingly obvious, "*I had to exhale*." Ah-ha! This simple revelation to the exercise is typically the first real lesson in spirituality for most individuals.

The root of spirituality, *spiritus*, comes from the Latin meaning "breath." Because it is so obvious, most individuals miss this point that we must exhale. It is, however, the key to our understanding of spirituality. It becomes clear that none of us can sustain ourselves by merely inhaling. We cannot be just in-spired. To survive, we *must* exhale. We have no choice in the matter. We are physiologically and biologically wired to inhale and exhale. Oxygen is exchanged for carbon dioxide. In the garden, the chemical transformation that occurs during photosynthesis is just the opposite as carbon dioxide is exchanged for oxygen as a by-product that we, as humans, need and use.

Simply put, we are connected to the breath. It contributes to the sustainability of other organisms in the environment. It is a relationship—it is reciprocal. That is spirituality. Think of this as spiritual photosynthesis. Spiritually (like plants) we need energy to create fuel that sustains us and creates a by-product that sustains others. The question to ponder here and now is two-fold: 1) what is it that sustains and fuels our spiritual self and; 2) what is the by-product of that process that in turn sustains others?

We often lose sight of that second question. Our society has conditioned us to focus on the first question and part of the process of the "inhaling" aspect of life is being "in-spired." The consumerist culture we live in tells us we will "sustain" ourselves and be much "happier" if we have this and that. The old computer programmer expression from years ago, "garbage in—garbage out," suggests that the quality of what we put into a program will have an effect of the final product. Similarly, we must consider if we are trying to fill our inner void with "garbage" in form of material toys and fads or with substantive things that nurture our spirit. Acquiring material things or a superficial lifestyle leaves most of us just as incomplete or empty. But as we discovered in our simple exercise, we cannot sustain ourselves by merely inhaling or by being "in-spired." We cannot only "take in" and expect to survive or be fulfilled.

Many people have long abandoned going to church because they didn't "_get_ anything out of it." This suggests an assumption that we must go to a place (church, mosque, synagogue, temple, zendo) as a repository of in-spiration. We sit in the pew waiting to acquire something—to be "in-spired" to live a better life, to gain insight into who we are and what is our place in the world. Often little or nothing happens.

The inability to become inspired is certainly not limited to religion. Some people seek inspiration from the arts by going to museums or concerts. Others retreat to nature as well. Each of these settings, like formal places of worship, can have a temporary or none at all. Any pursuit of becoming "in-spired" or seeking "in-spiration" in ANY setting is limiting when we have forgotten the reciprocal component of spirituality.

Eventually, we _must_ also exhale or give something back. We are transformed in this process of give and take when we relate to others. We are emotionally fulfilled when we live in a way that helps others as much as our self. Sadly, many individuals are stuck in jobs or careers that are not fulfilling often because it is difficult to see any meaningful "by-product" except a paycheck. The emptiness that so many people experience may stem from "gasping for air." How many of us have lives that are so busy and cluttered that we find ourselves saying we need to stop and "catch our breath?" That is not merely an expression. It accurately describes our need for spirituality. So what do we "take in" that we can "give back?" What do we need to sustain ourselves that we can also share to sustain others?

Reflection

How have you traditionally thought of "spirituality," and how has this passage impacted your understanding?

What sustains and fuels your spiritual self, and what is the by-product of that process that sustains others?

What spiritual roots do you draw from?

How do you or have you tried to fill any internal void you may have experienced?

Tips for Cultivating Your Spirituality

Inventory your gifts and talents that bring you great joy, and consider ways you can use them to help others in the community or in your church.

Regularly or routinely carve out time to go to places that "feed your soul" and spend some time there just sitting and thinking.

Prayer

Gracious God—
Remind us to breathe—to inhale and exhale—to take in and give back. Give us the energy and light to transform us internally so that we might transform the lives of others.

Amen

Chapter 7

Manure Happens: Desolation and Consolation

Seedlings for Thought:

The fairest thing in nature, a flower, still has its roots in earth and manure.

~ D.H. Lawrence

Scripture:

Luke 13:6-9 (New International Version)
Then he told this parable: "A man had a fig tree, planted in his vineyard, and he went to look for fruit on it, but did not find any. So he said to the man who took care of the vineyard, 'For three years now I've been coming to look for fruit on this fig tree and haven't found any. Cut it down! Why should it use up the soil?'" 'Sir,' the man replied, 'leave it alone for one more year, and I'll dig around it and fertilize it. If it bears fruit next year, fine! If not, then cut it down.'"

Hebrews 12:11 (New International Version)
No discipline seems pleasant at the time, but painful. Later on, however, it produces a harvest of righteousness and peace for those who have been trained by it.

*   *   *

As explored elsewhere on these pages, we know that soil can often become worn out. The dirt in a garden plot requires nutrients to be revitalized. Imagine vitamins for the earth, if you will. As noted in the scripture above, farmers and gardeners have long recognized the value of fertilizing crops. Today, we also have "high tech" and highly fortified chemically based fertilizers. These give burst of nitrogen and other nutrients that cause rapid growth —they also result in dependency on continual application and destruction of some of the beneficial microbes in the soil. Coincidently, many individuals are vitalized by a similar burst of spiritual ecstasy during a profound experience. It is, in every sense of the word, a "rush" that can energize us. But in time this momentary spiritual vitamin typically fades, often nudging us to find additional energy to sustain us.

The most basic and common type of fertilizer is manure, which farmers have been using for ages. After all, the fertilizer mentioned in the Bible was nothing but animal droppings. Somehow and somewhere in history, an attentive farmer noticed that something could actually grow up out of and from . . . well . . . crap. In a perverse sort of way, we can all take comfort in that fact. Unlike chemically based fertilizers, manure releases nutrients slowly throughout the growing season. It also supports microbes in the soil, and improves the soil's tilth, or workability. Manure lasts longer, but so does the stink. It is paradoxical that something as lovely and nurturing as a garden is actually dependent upon something so dirty and smelly. And unlike the shimmer and shine that come from chemically based fertilizers, manure is dirty, grimy, and smelly. There's not a whole lot of "shimmer" in the muck of manure. We tend to forget about or ignore this aspect of gardening as we harvest the bounty. In reality, it is manure that can facilitate such bounty. And in the process of spreading manure, the gardener invariably endures the less pleasant act and process of fertilizing the soil and crops, which is hard, heavy, and odiferous work! This tolerance is based on the knowledge and understanding that the nutrients found in this "waste material" are actually "good for the soil."

In some respects, we recognize that some of life's manure may be "good for the SOUL." To paraphrase a popular bumper sticker, "manure happens". It is highly unlikely we appreciate this fact at the moment manure happens in our lives. Naturally, we don't go looking for hardships, and, strangely, many individuals seem to experience more than their fair share of life's difficulties. That said, we tend to live in a very sanitized culture of happy endings and quick fixes bantered about in the media. Paradoxically, sometimes it is the muck we encounter that actually helps us grow . . . much like the stinky, dirty role of manure in the garden. Often, it takes time and hindsight to look back on the experience to recognize the dirty, messy, and smelly chapter of our own life story we had to wallow in that actually helped us grow.

Recognizing and appreciating the manure we experience is an example of what Ignatius of Loyola characterized as desolation. This is a moment when we don't necessarily feel the presence of God in our lives. Desolation is not a synonym for bad things or feelings. Instead, it is a moment of darkness that may actually shed light on aspects of our lives. Desolation can even bring us closer to God in some ways, as we long for God's care and protection. While a moment may bring discomfort because it's a dirty and smelly process, the experience may in fact make us stronger in the long run—much like the role of manure.

As parents and adults, we recognize that children and young people often have to learn life's lessons the hard way. Sometimes those lessons are best learned when, shall we say, the manure "hits the fan." This is what the second scripture from Hebrews alludes to. We mustn't confuse discipline with punishment, as we often do in contemporary society. In truth, it involves becoming a disciple of some thing or some one in order to learn and study. When discipline is a noun, it means a topic of study; when used as a verb, it means to persevere and study as an athlete who trains or a musician who practices. In order to grow, both the athlete and the musician must endure what is sometimes difficult or even painful. It means sacrifice.

In this case, we can see where discipline can be a metaphor for the manure that is heaped upon us. In gardening, the act of hauling and spreading something as heavy and stinky as manure is something to endure in order to reap the benefit of that nasty, smelly effort. You have to buck up, do it, get past it, and get over it, knowing it will produce decent soil and healthy crops. This is where consolation comes in.

It's easy for us to philosophize about life's hard lessons when it happens to someone else. It's more of a challenge when it is happening to us. We know that terrible and debilitating things happen to people. And in the grand scheme of things, the trials and tribulations we face often pale in comparison to others. They're still harder when they're ours. The scriptures are full of lamentations based on coping with and struggling with what life hands us. The entire book of Job is one long, big lesson on this topic. Job maintained patience and faith throughout his trials. And, according to scripture, he lived another 140 years: a long, good life. It is possible that this is because of all the "fertilizing" he endured.

Reflection

What times in your life have you had to deal with "manure"?

To what extent did this difficult time actually help nurture or "fertilize" your own personal growth? Were you aware of its potential benefit at that time, or did you come to this realization later? Or, might you still waiting to see how some difficulties could ever possibly nurture you?

Tips for Cultivating Your Spirituality

When you experience "manure" in your life, sit down and write yourself (and God) a letter about how you're feeling at the moment. Save the letter in a special place. Retrieve it in the future when you can reflect on the experience and how you feel now.

Make a list of your current troubles, difficulties, anxieties, and fears—consider writing each on a separate, small piece of paper. Offer each concern to God by either burying or burning each scrap of paper and concern as an act of prayer.

If you are experiencing a dark time, consider making a list of the contributing factors in one column. In a parallel column, jot down an opposite "glimmer of hope" to cling to across from each item.

Think of your own heroes or "she-roes" from scripture, history, or contemporary life. Contemplate the obstacles or challenges they encountered, and use this as an inspirational reminder of how these admired individuals persevered.

Thumb through Psalms, and find a passage of lamentation and a passage of hope to meditate on.

Find a companion who can gently hold and listen to your troubles without necessarily offering solutions or answers—a soul friend who can and will accompany you by listening non-judgmentally. Many churches have Stephen Ministers or spiritual directors who are willing to confidentially walk along side you through life's valleys, offering love, prayer, and listening; not giving advice or pity or pressure.

Prayer:

Gracious God—

There are times I feel so alone and down right crappy. It can seem like I'm stuck wallowing in dirty, smelly muck. The image of bright days, fragrant flowers, and the wonder of your creation seem can seem like a distant memory in times like these. Right now it may be hard to imagine how all of this struggle can possibly resolve itself, let alone make me stronger. Yet I know I'm not alone. You are with me. I know that from all of this I will grow and blossom into what you want me to be. But for now, just stay with me and hold me. Help me get out of this mess.

Amen

Chapter 8

Thank You Very Mulch:
Our Spiritual Security Blanket

Seedlings for Thought:

The glory of gardening: hands in the dirt, head in the sun, heart with nature. To nurture a garden is to feed not just on the body, but the soul. Share the botanical bliss of gardeners through the ages, who have cultivated philosophies to apply to their own—and our own—lives: Show me your garden and I shall tell you what you are.

~ Alfred Austin

Scripture:

Isaiah 4:6 (New International Version)
. . . It will be a shelter and shade from the heat of the day, and a refuge and hiding place from the storm and rain.

Psalm 5:11 (New International Version)
But let all who take refuge in you be glad; let them ever sing for joy. Spread your protection over them, that those who love your name may rejoice in you.

*   *   *

The U.S. Department of Agriculture defines mulch as a protective layer of material spread over the soil. A gardener will scatter material around and in between crops to help protect it from the elements. Naturally, a garden requires water to survive, but too much rain or driving rain can actually harm the crops. Mulch protects the soil from erosion and reduces compaction from the impact of heavy rains. At the same time, mulch also conserves moisture, reducing the need for frequent watering. Mulch maintains even temperature in the soil. On the hottest summer day, a gardener can poke a finger down through mulch and feel moist, cool dirt. It retains moisture and buffers intense heat and light from the sun. Conversely, mulch can protect the ground when there is a sudden cold snap. Mulch helps maintains a nice balance of hot and cold, wet and dry. Too much of any one condition can be problematic. Finally, mulch minimizes weeds. This protective layer keeps weeds from sprouting and stealing the soil's nutrients that our crops need. An added benefit is that less time and energy is spent on weeding, allowing the gardener more time to do other "more fun" gardening tasks. We can almost think of mulch as the garden's security blanket. This protective blanket allows the crops to grow and be all they can be.

Mulch can often be composed of a variety of materials. While these mulching materials may effective, they require manufactured materials. Many large gardens and farms use rolls and rolls of plastic or light fabric, which cost money to make, to buy, and sometimes even to remove. Plastic, for example, is petroleum-based product. Additionally, this artificial mulch must be retrieved and disposed of either into landfills or recycling centers.

Natural or organic mulch is a great alternative for a number of reasons. One is economic, as you can use existing waste materials that don't cost anything. Examples include wood chips, grass clippings, leaves, shredded newspaper, or straw. There are other advantages as well. This type of organic mulch has the added benefit of breaking down into the soil, adding nutrients. There is nothing to remove, dispose of, or recycle. The point is that the protective layer can comprise many things, including materials that seem like "waste," such as dried, dead leaves. This shows that there is more than one way to provide protection that promotes healthy growth.

Our task and challenge is to look for ways in our own lives that will serve as our "spiritual mulch." As we go through each day, we too are often battered about by the "elements." Like the hot sun beating down on fragile seedlings, we may need some shade so that the life is not baked out of us. How many times do we use the adjective "fried" to describe our state of being? Our busy and frenetic lives seem to lock us in a pressure cooker of schedules, tasks, and activities to the point we feel like we're about to blow. Conversely, many of us feel more and more instability that erodes the foundation of our personal lives. We run the risk of being washed away when life's thunderstorms come pouring in. We also need something to wrap around ourselves to keep intrusions, such as life's weeds, at bay. These are the pesky and non-essential things in life that take time, energy, and nutrients from us. Our "mulch blanket" also keeps us warm, safe, secure, and holds in what sustains us. Just as an attentive gardener knows this and regularly applies mulch to crops, we need to create layers of security around our loved ones and us.

Unfortunately, the approach or materials we typically incorporate as a kind of spiritual mulch are often manufactured, much like the sheets of plastic fabric some gardeners use. We spend a lot of time, money, and energy creating or buying what we believe or hope to be a spiritual security blanket. We assume buying this new gadget or toy will ward off feelings of inadequacy and revive our worn out life. Instead, these objects require additional time, energy, and cost to maintain them. Sometimes they accumulate in the closet, attic, or garage. Other times they clutter our homes and lives, merely taking up physical and spiritual space without actually being "mulch-like" at all.

It's not always "stuff" that we use to provide that protection and security we need. We may invest time and money into activities, classes, workshops, and seminars, which can certainly enrich our lives, but only up to a certain point. Instead of enhancing our lives, many of us run ourselves ragged dashing from one event to the next, often distracting us from what we truly want and need. Ironically, our lives spin out of control because of a lack of balance—too much or too little of anything throws us out of spiritual equilibrium. And yet mulch is a rather simple way of maintaining balance. Mulch helps maintain temperature and moisture when it's *too* hot or cold or dry or wet. Notice that mulch does not necessarily keep these climatic calamities from happening—it merely serves as protection that helps bring balance. The key word here is "balance."

Our search for this spiritual security blanket does not always involve stuff or activities. Like some gardeners who use synthetics to "protect" their crops, we may apply chemicals to ward off emotional weeds that infiltrate our spiritual security. Our culture, like our huge macro-agribusiness, looks to chemicals to "solve our problems." Many individuals turn to alcohol, tobacco, prescribed drugs, and other substances under the illusion they will help us evade the threatening elements life throws at us. Instead, the chemicals merely numb or distract us temporarily. So what can we use as natural spiritual mulch in our lives?

We need to remember the core of spirituality is relationships—relationships with our self, others, God's creation, and with God. So, focusing on the way we relate and interact with key people in our lives is good place to start. A life partner, family member, a dear friend can help sustain us when our lives are out of balance. We also have to make time for ourselves and nurture our own growth just as we would a seedling in the garden. This self-care includes physical and emotional attention. Again, we need to balance our self-care with care for others so we don't become preoccupied with our own needs at the expense of others. We also need to consider the activities we indulge in and ponder to what extent they provide the spiritual security blanket we need. How much television, video games, recreational activities, classes and seminars do we engage in and how much of that truly nurtures our spirit? In contrast, how much time do we invest in reading inspirational and uplifting works? In serving others?

Reflection

What or who serves as mulch in your life that helps nurture your growth while at the same protects you from the exposure to harmful elements?

What are some of the "elements" in your own experience and life that you need to balance?

What are some potentially harmful "elements" you need some protection from?

What are some examples of artificial mulch you've used in the past that you thought might serve as your spiritual security blanket but didn't?

Likewise and as stated in the passage from Psalms at the beginning of this passage, in what ways do we provide mulch to others to protect them allow their lives to sing and grow?

Tips for Cultivating Your Spirituality

Spirituality is about relationships and we can draw comfort from relationships. Likewise, those we know and love can draw comfort from us. Take a moment and write a note of thanks and affirmation to a loved one who provides security and safety to you. Tell them how much their friendship means to you. Your own well-being is nurtured by affirming others.

We all experience dark times. Take time now during lighter, good times to make a list of people, activities, and places that provide a sense of security and comfort. Keep the list in a safe place and refer to it in dark, unsure times. Seek the security of those people, places, and things that nurture your soul rather than resort to artificial or chemical sources.

Prayer

Gracious God—

You are my security blanket that protects me. I take comfort and refuge in your strength. Give me the wisdom to surround myself with constructive people, thoughts, and lifestyle. Remind me that I, too, provide safety and security to others in their times of need. Let me be mindful of those who are going through life without the necessary support and security that I am blessed with. Lead me through each day knowing that I may un-knowingly provide glimpses and moments of security to others through the way I live.

Amen

Chapter 9

Crop Rotation: Preventing Spiritual Blight

Seedling for Thought:

To cultivate a garden is to walk with God.

~ Christian Nestell Bovee

Scripture:

1 Corinthians 12:4-6
There are different kinds of gifts, but the same Spirit. There are different kinds of service, but the same Lord. There are different kinds of working, but the same God works all of them in all individuals.

*   *   *

Many inexperienced gardeners plant the same crop in the same place in the same plot year after year. Unknowingly, this practice endangers the garden for a number of reasons. One is that the same crop tends to wear out the soil. Rotating the crops we plant in a given area balances the fertility of the soil. Crop rotation is necessary to minimize the possibility of infestation by fungus, virus, insects, and other pests that can acclimate to the setting and threaten growth. The potato famine in Ireland was the result of blight—not diversifying and not rotating. This condition had a devastating ripple effect resulting in human starvation.

We risk the threat of "spiritual blight" when we lock ourselves into a rut of worship or spiritual practice. The process may lose its meaning over time. This is a common occurrence within worship services themselves. And while we can draw comfort in the familiar, we can also run the risk of mechanizing worship so that it loses its meaning over time.

When asked what was the greatest commandment (Mark 12:29-30), Christ cited the Shema (pronounced: shmah) from the Hebrew law found in Deuteronomy 6: 4-5 that we are to love God with our heart, mind, soul, and might (which can be thought of as through our work with our hands or deeds). We are careful to note that the act of loving, worshiping and being with God is not limited to a single way. The scripture does not command us to choose between using our heart OR our mind OR our might. It emphatically uses the conjunction "and" meaning there is more than one way to worship, love, and be with God. In fact, it would serve us well to remember that Christ himself used many ways to nurture his own spirituality. He sought quiet mediation and prayer (Matthew 14:23). He healed the sick and disabled (John 5:5-9). Even as a child, he used His mind when He engaged in intellectual study of the scripture with church leaders (Luke 2:46-47). He taught and gave sermons (Matthew 5) and gathered together with others for fellowship that included eating together (John 21:4-13).

We are taught in 1 Corinthians 12 that each of us has gifts that can be used in different ways to serve others as a form of community and worship.

And we can tap into these same gifts and talents as a way of nurturing our own spirituality while nurturing the spirituality of others. Likewise, it is important to tap into those gifts of others to balance the things we cannot do ourselves. Even in the Old Testament, we read that the artists crafted works of art to be used during worship (Exodus 31:3-5). We are reminded to sing songs of praise—not just the same old songs, but new ones (Psalms 33). Even fasting can be a way of worship and nurturing our spiritual growth (Acts 13:20).

Like rotating crops to minimize the possibility of blight, rotating or practicing an array of spiritual exercises minimizes the risk of "spiritual blight" in which we get stuck in a rut or habit so that our spirituality loses its meaning. This variety maintains and nurtures our own spiritual fertility as well as an ability to grow and blossom. Otherwise, we run the risk that "pests" from our everyday lives may infiltrate and contaminate our spiritual growth. We can become preoccupied with the mundane and the routine, forgetting to celebrate the wonders of the world and our lives. Analogous to the inexperienced gardener, many of us tend to nurture our spiritual growth through routine. Nothing is inherently wrong with routine, as it can lead to habits that help us sustain our spirituality. Over time, however, the familiar and comfortable can become *so* routine that we risk losing the meaning as we merely go through the motions of an exercise. Theologian, Urban T. Holmes refers to this as "acedia," or spiritual boredom. Going to worship services (and even sitting in the same pew) or setting aside time in the morning for devotion and meditation is a good thing and something to continue. And as in our example of improving the soil's fertility to promote plant growth, adding to, or modifying our spiritual practice can nurture our spiritual growth. We can keep our worship and spirituality fertile by trying different forms of spiritual practice or exercise using our minds, heart, and hands. We can use an intellectual approach by reading a book on spirituality or attending a lecture or workshop. We can nurture an artistic approach by listening to music or reading poetry or even watching provocative films that speak to our soul. We can volunteer to do some service with a local non-profit organization. We can sit with others for coffee and fellowship.

There are so many ways to nurture our soul and spirit. Trying something new may revive your spirituality and introduce you to a whole new spiritual practice.

Reflection

What are the consistent ways you nurture your spirituality and relationship with God? To what extent do these activities continue to enrich the soil from which your own spirituality grows, or have these activities become mundane and routine?

What is the difference between a "routine" and a "rut"? Can you name some of your routines and ruts?

What new ways or approaches might you consider? How might you use the head, heart, and hands to not only serve God, but to provide spiritual nutrients to your own spiritual grounding?

Think of a time you attended church and you experienced something entirely new. Did it surprise you? Did it make you uncomfortable and if so, why? Has there ever been a time you experienced a something out of the ordinary, either in worship or in your life that revived your soul and spirit? If so, what was it and why do you think it had that effect on you? Are there ways to replicate that experience?

Tips for Cultivating Your Spirituality

Consider ways to use and expand your knowledge and understanding of God and your own spirituality by searching for books, films, lectures, or essays. Find an author or particular academic resource that resonates with you and intellectually cultivate your spirituality. Check your church or local library to borrow materials. Form a book and/or film club to join in fellowship with kindred spirits to collectively explore and ponder your spirituality

Likewise, think about the various forms of art that might be used to cultivate your spiritual growth. Explore music, poetry, artwork, crafts, or dance that speak to your heart. Spend time with these artistic expressions as a form of mediation and prayer. Let God speak to you through these works of art.

Research the various mission projects at your own congregation or service opportunities within your community. Find a cause or organization that appeals to you and spend time with your hands to serve others "with all your might" as a form of living out your spirituality.

Spend time in and with nature. Feel God's presence in God's glorious creation. Hike, ride a bike, or just sit on a rock to take in the splendor of the world around you.

Consider visiting another church within or outside your denomination or even a synagogue or mosque to experience other ways the "families of Abraham" worship God to gain insight into a new spiritual perspective.

The communal act of eating with others can be a way to nurture your spirituality. Consider ways to organize and schedule regular gatherings of friends to share meals. Conversely, think about the practice of fasting as a way to cultivate your personal spirituality.

Prayer

Gracious God—

Much of our life is spent in a rut. Worshiping and spending time with you should not contribute to our own sense of spiritual blight or boredom. Enliven us to use the many gifts and ways to celebrate you and to love you. Help us creatively rotate our spirituality that renews us and sustains us. We can broaden our spiritual horizons by exploring new ways to know you, to worship you, and to spend time with you. It is easy for us to become lazy or mechanize our spiritual lives to the point it all loses its meaning. We pledge to renew our spirit in a variety of ways that helps us love you with all our mind, heart, soul, and might.

Amen

Chapter 10

Compost: Transformation and New Life

Seedlings for Thought

My whole life has been spent waiting for an epiphany, a manifestation of God's presence—the kind of transcendent, magical experience that lets you see your place in the big picture. And this is what I had with my first compost heap.

~ Bette Midler

Gardens bring us into contact with the cycles and irrefutable laws of nature, teaching us indelible lessons about ourselves and about the messy, difficult, and beautiful processes of living.

~ Cait Johnson

Scripture

2 Corinthians 5:17 (New International Version)
Therefore, if anyone is in Christ, he is a new creation; the old has gone, the new has come!

*   *   *

Most folks don't give a whole lot of thought to compost. However, some gardeners not only think about it, they are obsessed by it! If the average person on the street were asked to define compost the responses would probably include something like, "waste material." Some might take it a step further to say the "waste" is "re-cycled into making something else." Both of these responses are correct and there are some important spiritual factors buried in there. But before we dive into that, let's be sure we have a basic understanding of what compost is and how it is used.

Compost has been around for a long, long time. The concept and process of composting is actually alluded to in Genesis 3:19 with the familiar passage, "ashes to ashes, dust to dust." The University of Illinois Extension Office notes that compost was described and used 1,000 years before Moses during the ancient Akkadian Empire in Mesopotamia. Also, there are documents written 200 years before Christ by a Roman General Marcus Procius Cato who described how to use compost. Pliney the Elder refers to compost in the first century after Christ. And yes, compost is waste. In a nutshell, compost is a chemical process in which waste organic material decomposes and is transformed into soil. The organic material actually heats up and basically "cooks." On cool days, steam rises from the compost pile so it is warm when you put your hand in it. The heat kills off harmful bacteria, while other microorganisms help aerate what has now become dirt and ward off various diseases that could be harmful to plants. Chemically speaking, it is a combination of nitrogen, carbon, air, and water. The decomposition process enriches and enlivens the soil that ultimately helps other things grow. A third of the "recipe" is composed of green or colorful stuff (like grass, green plants or kitchen scraps) that are full of nitrogen. The other two-thirds is made up of brown and dry stuff that is full of carbon. About 30% to 50% of household food waste is loaded with nitrogen and carbon that can be converted into compost. This reduces what goes into landfills AND . . . it's all natural. To facilitate the transformation process, the layered pile must be stirred up and turned to allow air in. If it is not, the pile becomes an anaerobic, smelly sludge that prevents the beneficial microorganisms from doing their work.

All of this properly composted "waste" is transformed into beautiful, rich, fertile, black soil that can be used to grow amazing food. If the gardener does not add compost to the garden, the soil becomes depleted. The patch of dirt is no longer able to support garden life. It depends on this "used up stuff" to support new life. So much for this history and biology lesson—what does compost have to do with nurturing our spirituality?

First, let's think about "waste" for a moment—what does that mean? Webster's Dictionary defines waste as a *by-product process of gradual loss or decrease of a product from use, scrap, refuse or an un-wanted by—product*. It could be thought of as something that has been "used up" or "exhausted," giving it no further value and therefore tossed away. Many people feel exhausted or used up. Referring to one of the opening quotes of this passage, these individuals have experienced the messy and difficult process of living and they're just plain tired. They have no further purpose or value as they are simply spent. This is a sad but true reality for many—perhaps for you. But like the composting process, adding and mixing up some other elements can rejuvenate life. It requires some work to pile, turn, stir, and mix it up as the process begins to heat up and cook. The beauty of composting is that what seems to be used up or wasted is almost miraculously transformed into something else.

Curiously, out of a similar kind of spiritual death, elements are actually transformed into a whole new life and purpose. In an odd sort of way, composting is symbolic of the resurrection—something that has been used up comes back to life in another form. Often we mourn the passing aspects of our lives—our children grow up and leave, a loved one dies, we leave behind our youth for careers, we leave behind careers for retirement, our physical bodies change. And while it may seem that those cherished things from our lives have come and gone, in actuality, they have simply evolved into something new. As our children grow and leave us, we are no longer merely parents, but grandparents as well. As we exit a career, we now have insight that can be useful as we mentor the next generation of professionals. Christ embodied this notion of "new life" through his crucifixion and resurrection. Through living a Christ-like life, we, too are transformed and given new life.

Second, composting uses natural, rather than synthetic components. It is interesting that our contemporary culture and society attempts to use "artificial" things to help us restore our depleted lives. Even gardening and farming have been inundated with petroleum-based fertilizers, herbicides and pesticides with the promise of "improving" our harvest. Over time, we are essentially ingesting oil into our diet.

We are encouraged to buy this or that with the promise and hope that it will renew us. We accumulate more and more stuff assuming it will somehow transform an otherwise empty life into something substantial. We are taught that getting and acquiring stuff will sustain us. Ironically, in composting the opposite is true. It is the decomposition of "stuff" that has sustenance. The collection of natural elements is transformed to sustain and enrich the soil from which healthy food emerges that, in turn, physically sustains us. The same thing can occur when we metaphorically collect natural or real aspects of life rather than manufactured objects. Friends, travel, the arts, exercise, quiet reflection, and even working in a garden are all natural elements and activities that can transform and emotionally sustain us. It is these things, not artificial or manufactured components that can nurture our souls and spirit.

Finally, we are reminded that we are intimately connected to the earth. The Hebrew word *Adamah* means "of the earth" and from where the name "Adam" comes. All life, including us, is carbon-based. And as the scripture in Genesis reminds us, eventually we will return to the earth. Watching and working with compost reminds us of the mystery and miracle of the cycle of life. It's good for the garden, too!

Reflection

In what ways have aspects of your life "died" and yet come back to new life in another form? What are some natural transitions or cycles of life you've experienced or witnessed in your own life or family? How do you recognize, understand, or appreciate the role and purpose of that cycle of life—of transforming from one thing to another?

In what ways can you nurture aspects of your life that have been used up in ways that will transform into something else or new in your life?

What are some facets of your life from the past that you might revive or "resurrect" to give your spirit new life?

Do you feel "wasted" or "used up" or "exhausted"? What has led you to this state or condition? What would revive your spirit? What things in your past used to feed your soul that might possibly be resurrected to give you new life or purpose?

Are you holding on to things (material, activities, people) that no longer give you sustenance? Do they create a rotting, smelly, stagnating mess that needs to be turned, aired out, and allowed to decompose in a healthy manner?

Tips for Cultivating Your Spiritual

Take inventory of phases, events, and interests in your life. Acknowledge those that have "run their course." Celebrate them and let them go, allowing yourself to evolve into something else and something new.

Consider past interests, skills, talents, roles and responsibilities. Ponder how they might be re-conceptualized or revised into something similar, breathing new life into the past.

Make a list of past trials and transgressions that you allow to haunt you or follow you. Take your list outside and burn it in a safe setting, then bury the ashes to send those ghosts from the past on their way. Let them go and say a prayer.

Go through your stuff. If you haven't used the item(s) in the past two years, give it a new life by giving it away to someone who might actually be able to use it.

Mix up your life a bit and let it cook up by trying something new—a new hobby, place to go, different kind of food or cooking. Mixing novelty with the status quo may heat up your stagnant life into something new.

Prayer

Gracious God—

There are days I feel totally used up. I have little to no energy. Breathe new life into me so that I may be of service to myself, to others, and to You. With each day, I am born again into something new. Thank you for my daily re-birth. And with each closing chapter of my life story, give me the strength, courage, and insight to evolve into something new.

Amen

Chapter 11

Pests: Spiritual Locusts & Sin

<u>Seedling for Thought:</u>

On every stem, on every leaf, . . . and at the root of everything that grew, was a professional specialist in the shape of grub, caterpillar, aphid, or other expert, whose business it was to devour that particular part.

~ Oliver Wendell Holmes

<u>Scripture:</u>

Malachi 3:11
"I will prevent pests from devouring your crops, and the vines in your fields will not drop their fruit before it is ripe," says the LORD Almighty.

*   *   *

Webster's dictionary defines a pest as *a plant or animal detrimental to humans or human concerns*. The Online Etymological Dictionary traces the word back to the 1600s when its use meant a *"noxious or troublesome person or thing."* So a pest is anything or any person that distracts us from something or someone that is important and worthy of our attention.

There are three steps in dealing with garden pests. First, the gardener must be aware of a possibility that something may be threatening the crops.

The second step involves noticing things that can often be small signs. Awareness is not enough, as the gardener must now intentionally look, probe, and examine the soil and leaves. Finally, when the gardener does observe evidence of some kind of infestation, a response is required. Simply hoping it will go away or ignoring it won't help. The plant will be ruined and the entire garden may be at risk if the pest is menacing enough. A marauding deer can turn a garden into its own personal salad bar.

The gardener has some effective ways to keep pests from nibbling away at the garden. Integrated pest management promotes natural controls, such as owls, wasps, and ladybugs. When the soil and plants are healthy, pests are less likely to do much damage. When infestations do occur, concocting natural pesticides consisting of water, garlic, and chili pepper can be sprayed on plants to keep aphids away without harm or any lingering taste. Planting certain colorful flowers attracts the "good bugs" that eat the "bad bugs." Not only does this approach protect the crops, it adds a splash of color to the garden bed. Netting or small mesh fencing can also be used to keep birds or deer out of the garden. Battery operated vibrating "spikes" can be embedded into the ground to minimize tunneling by gophers. Finally, when more drastic measures are required, traps might be employed to control gophers or moles.

In gardening, we are focused on the produce with the goal of growing and harvesting our crops. When pests invade our garden—gophers, aphids, mold, marauding birds, and deer—we shift our attention away from directly tending to the crops. This is a necessary evil, as we cannot ignore these pests, due to the damage they cause. In fact, some pests may actually take over the garden. We now spend time, money, and energy on these darn distractions when we'd much rather devote ourselves to nurturing the growth of our crops. And some might argue that we are, in fact, *indirectly* tending to the garden when we fight off pests. After all, we are essentially caring for the garden by defending it. While there is truth to that, the effort is expending negative, rather than positive, energy.

All of us have experienced negative energy in our family lives or work lives. It is when we spend considerable time and resources *reacting* to a problem—a behavior, debt, and illness—in an effort to make it go away. That is a good thing as it is an intentional act to improve or "fix" something. It is vital to respond rather than let the situation worsen, only to require even more resources and energy later. That same energy could have been shifted from *reacting* to a *problem* to *proactively creating* something new.

The same is true as we tend to our spirituality. We must be cognizant of the "pests" that can invade our spiritual and personal lives. At best, these spiritual pests become annoying distractions that shift our time and energy away from how we relate to our self, others, and God. At worst, these pests can take over life just as they can take over a garden. Some of the pests overtly manifest themselves as addictions. But there are other subtler, and therefore perhaps even more insidious pests that creep into our lives. These include out-of-control spending and consumerism, over-working at jobs, mindless TV viewing or web-surfing, constant communication through texting, emails, or cell phones, maintaining an image or reputation, climbing the company ladder—the list goes on and on. These behaviors in and of themselves are inherently not bad or wrong. It is when they, as we see in Webster's definition, become detrimental to humans or human concerns that they become pests and run the risk of taking over.

In addition to the array of outward circumstances and behaviors that can become pests, we have the inner pests that distract us from having positive, constructive relationships with others and with God. Like many pests in the garden, we can't always see what is wreaking all that havoc, but we know it's there. It takes some close-up examination to notice the tiny aphids gnawing away on leaves. Likewise, we sometimes need to take a close and deep look at what is gnawing away at our spirit and is keeping us from relating to others and to God. Admittedly, this can be an intimidating process. We don't have to do this on our own. A spiritual director can be of use in this process. A spiritual director is, as Margaret Guenther describes, a companion with another person as they experience God's grace on their own spiritual journey. It is the responsibility of the spiritual director to provide tools or pathways for persons as they come to understand their relationship with God. It is not psychotherapy or pastoral counseling. A spiritual director listens and reflects what is heard back to the individual creating that important prerequisite step of awareness. There is an array of spiritual exercises or practices that might be offered through spiritual direction, most of which come from a rich tradition that can assist in noticing ways that help keep our inner pests at bay.

Theologian John Neafsey suggested that sin is the personal pursuit of something that contradicts the purposes of God. Throughout the passages in this book, we are reminded that from the very beginning of time, God has been The Gardener of our Earth. God's purpose was to create this wonderful place with wonderful creatures caring for that place and each other. When we shift our attention away from caring for this world and those inhabiting it, we engage in the personal pursuit of something that contradicts the purpose of God—that is, we sin. It is relatively easy to look at our stereotypical list of sins and absolve ourselves from any guilt in committing the "biggies" such as murder, adultery, or stealing and the like and then walk away feeling pretty good about ourselves. But in the big scheme of things, sin is when life's pests distract us, keeping us from tending to "*the* garden." The garden can be our own personal growth, our family, our community, or the global community. We must be aware of, and diligent in fending off things that distract us from using positive energy that promotes growth and harvest in those settings. We must notice and name the pests that distract us from our relationships with our self, others, and God. Once we have done that, we have to apply some "spiritual pesticide" to keep those pests at bay.

These "spiritual pesticides" are really just spiritual exercises that can take many forms and formats. Many of us have preconceived notions of what spiritual exercises are or look like. These include devotional readings and writing journals, but these certainly are not the only exercises. Furthermore, these may not work or resonate with some individuals. Curiously, many of us just work too hard at this. As mentioned above, the initial steps only require awareness and noticing. All that means is stopping what we're doing to discover what we are thinking, feeling, and doing in the way we relate to our self, others, and God. That's it. Nothing more. It can be done almost anywhere and at any time for just a few minutes. This is where and when we begin to notice our blessings as well as the "pests" nibbling away at our spirit. Something has caught our attention saying, "Hey, notice me!" We can choose to ignore it and hope it will go away, or we can respond. Otherwise, we run the risk of these pests taking over our lives just as they can take over a garden.

Reflection

What are some of the "gardens" in your life that require tending? What is it in each of these gardens you are hoping to cultivate?

When and how are you aware of "pests" in your spiritual and personal life?

What are some of the "pests" in your personal and spiritual life that may distract you?

How do you typically contend with or control those pests (if at all)?

What is your notion of sin? Has it changed after reading this passage and if so, why or how?

What are your notions of spiritual exercises? Which, if any, do you practice? How effective are they?

To what extent do you stop and take notice? How? When? Where?

Tips For Cultivating Your Spirituality

Take a walk or just sit somewhere. Notice what comes to mind. After a few minutes, jot down as many of those thoughts as you can. Review the list and see what patterns might emerge. What is that list telling you? What "pests" or "blessings" may emerge?

Sit down and make two columns on a piece of paper. In the left column, make a list of all the "pests" in your spiritual and personal life. In the right column, ponder and list possible ways to "control" those pests.

Go to your public or church library and peruse the shelf for books on spirituality or devotionals. Consider using one for 15 minutes a day as a devotional reader.

Check with your church to find groups that might help you tend to your own spiritual garden. Some of these groups are devoted to study. Other groups are designed to help participants nurture their spirituality.

Look for volunteer service opportunities at your church or in the local newspaper. Notice what you're thinking and feeling before, during, and after the service.

Consider finding a spiritual director. The initial meeting is always a discussion of the process and an exploration to see if there's a good match between the two of you. Check with your church or the directory of spiritual directors on the website of Spiritual Directors International for a list of directors in your area.

Prayer

Gracious God—

I'm so tired of swatting at all of life's annoyances that distract me from tending the garden in my life. Gently lead me to a quiet still place to take note of these spiritual pests so I can find the time and the will to address each one. Give me the strength and patience to endure the ones that can't or don't seem to go away. Give me the insight to recognize the pests that loved ones and total strangers are wrestling with, and provide me with the love and patience to support them.

Amen

Chapter 12

Of the World: Climate and Environment

Seedling for Thought

Weather is a great metaphor for life—sometimes it's good, sometimes it's bad, and there's nothing much you can do about it but carry an umbrella.

~ Terri Guillemets

Scripture

Luke 12:54-55
He said to the crowd: "When you see a cloud rising in the west, immediately you say, 'It's going to rain,' and it does. And when the south wind blows, you say, 'It's going to be hot,' and it is . . ."

*　　*　　*

In addition to having good soil as its foundation, a garden must have an environment that is conducive to growth. And not all environments are the same—each has its quirks. A gardener in Phoenix, Arizona must know and do things differently from a gardener in Duluth, Minnesota, due to their different climatic conditions. Gardens *can* be planted in extreme climatic conditions, but when they are, the gardener is keenly aware of the extra special attention and effort that are required.

Ideally, we *choose* where to plant a garden, selecting a space with adequate sunlight and water. Hopefully, the climate itself is not too harsh, requiring significant structures and/or resources like green houses or large amounts of water to sustain the garden. But we may not be able to do much about the climatic environment. We may actually be stuck. However, we can read the climatic conditions of any environment and respond to it.

As we tend to the garden of our lives, we must also take notice of and respond to the environmental conditions we find ourselves in. Obviously, our spiritual lives are more likely to prosper in settings conducive to growth. Challenging circumstances and surroundings can have a disruptive and potential damaging impact. There's not a whole lot we can do about the weather or the climatic conditions of where we live. We can, however, take note in ways that allow us to prepare as much as we can and respond to whims of the environment we find ourselves in. The opening quote and scripture are really talking about reading the signs of the times and knowing when and how to respond. The gardener must read the weather and know how to respond. Tender seedlings must be covered when there is the risk of an impending frost. When the weather is hot and dry, the gardener must supply the water in lieu of much needed rain.

We must take stock of our settings and evaluate how they may impact us. Do we put ourselves in the midst of noise, distractions, and clutter either physically or figuratively? Or are we in calm surroundings that nurture our personal and spiritual lives?

If we stop to think about it, weather is the result of many factors. Moisture in the air, temperature, winds, pressure systems, and geographical location combine in various amounts to create climate. Our lives are the same. The combination of factors surrounding us creates the condition we find ourselves in. Some conditions we can do little or nothing about. But there are some things we can do to influence the other factors and elements swirling around us. We actually have some choices here and there. The astute gardener chooses plants that will thrive in their climate. An English cottage garden is vastly different from a desert xeriscaped garden. Choosing whom we spend time with, based on their values and behaviors, can make either us wither or help us thrive. In the cases where we do have choices and control, it is incumbent upon us to make intentional decisions. We can usually choose the type of people we want to associate with. What are their attitudes toward life? What are their values? How do they spend time? Those people shape who we are and who we become.

We can also typically choose where and how to spend a good portion of our time. Are we in front of the TV or computer screen? And if so, what are we watching and what impact does it have? Are we waiting for life to come to us or are we going out looking for life? Do we spend all our time working, wearing out our bodies and spirit, or do we take a time out now and then? Do we sit alone, cocooned in our own house and life, or do we explore and interact with others?

We can choose whether to be proactive and take care of our bodies through exercise and diet. We can choose how we want to spend our money. These choices have an impact on us and on the way we live.

But, even in these examples, there are some constraining factors we have no control over. We often find ourselves dealing with conflict—whether in the garden or in our lives. Conflict can be thought of as a situation in which our goals are not being met. Regardless of the goal or the circumstances that inhibit us from attaining our goal, there is one thing we DO have control over and that is how we respond. We can become angry. We can throw a fit. We can cry. We can give up. We can think about our options and available resources to try a different approach. Therefore our only option is to respond accordingly. Just as the gardener observes and responds to the weather, we can look at the gathering conditions of our lives and try to anticipate what is about to unfold and prepare as much as we can.

Admittedly, sometimes things in the garden and our in lives just don't go our way and there is little or nothing we can do to prevent what unfolds. The gardener can do little about a hailstorm that batters crops to pieces, except to surrender to it and start over. Luckily, there are times when others like family and friends—sometimes total strangers—come to our rescue. These are some of the human resources available to us and that we can surround ourselves with. This is a two-way street. To what extent do we avail ourselves to others? How is the way we live our life contributing to the environmental conditions of others? Our spirituality is based on relationships—how we relate with others and the world around us. How we respond and relate to something outside our self has an impact on us. Likewise, how we go about responding to those conditions both within us and outside us will influence our outcomes. We can plop ourselves down in the middle of a garden plot—or our life—wringing our hands lamenting there is little we can do to influence those sprouts or we can look around us and within us to make choices on how to respond to our environments. Simply put, we can heed the cloudy skies and take an umbrella with us, knowing we might end up not needing it, or we can take our chances and get soaked.

Reflection

Who are the people you spend time with? What effect do they have on you? What choices do you have regarding the people you are around?

Where do you spend a good deal of your time? What effect do these settings have on you? What choices do you have in modifying where you spend your time?

How do you spend your time? What are some choices or alternatives to how you spend your time?

To what extent do you look around the setting and circumstances of your life to predict and proactively take steps to minimize potential problems and conflict as well as maximize opportunities for growth? Or are you a spectator of your own life?

How do you typically respond to conflict? Do you place blame on others? Do you think about how to respond? Do you lash out? Do you withdraw? What is the effect of how you respond to conflict? What does the way you respond to conflict reveal about yourself?

To what extent are you "there" for others? When was the last time you came to the rescue or assistance of someone else? What was the circumstance that seemed to trigger your response? How did you feel afterwards?

Tips for Cultivating Your Spirituality

On a weekly calendar, make hourly boxes for each day. Jot down how you typically spend each hour of the day. Review and reflect on the calendar. Consider what your calendar is telling you about how you spend your time. Are you way too busy? Or are you flitting time away on things that may not be responsive to the needs and condition of the setting your find yourself in?

Weather forecasting is a scientific method of looking at how all the surrounding conditions combine to create an expected result. Conduct your own spiritual forecast by looking at all the surrounding conditions in your life that nurture your spirituality.

Make a list of all your blessings and resources. Make a list of things you can control and not control. Make a list or menu of choices can you make in your life that will help your own spiritual garden thrive.

Prayer

Gracious God—
You have given us so much. Sometimes we take these gifts for granted and don't use them as we should. One of our gifts is using the common sense you gave us to make good choices. Open our eyes and minds to recognize and utilize our gifts. Help us read the signs of the times in our lives and respond according to your will.

Amen

Chapter 13

Harvest: Reap What You Sow

Seedling for Thought

Anytime I am looking to somebody else as my source, I'm coming from scarcity. I am no longer trusting God, or the Universe, for my harvest. It's reasonable for me to have expectations based on what somebody I trust has committed to. And it's natural for me to feel disappointed when that somebody doesn't come through. But when I feel more than disappointment, when I also feel anger, it's because I deviated from my truth. It's because I compromised my truth to get what somebody else promised. Because when I'm really following my truth, I will be at peace with the consequences—whatever they are. I can accept somebody else's truth, but I must live my own truth.

~ Jan Denise

Scripture

Psalm 107:37
They sowed fields and planted vineyards that yielded a fruitful harvest . . .

*   *   *

Harvest is the culmination of everything that has been presented in these passages. It should seem somewhat obvious that a gardener will not harvest any crops unless there is a place to grow the seeds with good soil, and then tending the plants with compost, mulch, staking, weeding, and watering. Harvesting is the literal "take away."

Harvesting potatoes is a lot like digging for treasure. The gardener slides the shovel or pitch fork into the earth and turns the soil over to uncover wonderful nuggets clustered together around the roots of the plant. It is the closest thing to playing for a gardener.

Every once in a while, a single stray plant called a "volunteer" will spring up out of nowhere. This is the result of a seed being accidentally scattered and taking root. The plant "voluntarily" produces not only food, but also a little extra bonus to harvest. It is one of life's little surprises. Unlike the typical consumer who seeks cosmetically perfect produce, the gardener knows that good food does not always look pretty. Sometimes the produce takes an odd shape, giving it a unique appearance that would be rejected by commercial growers.

Back in the days before commercial gardening, the conscientious gardener not only harvested produce, but the seeds from the produce. Collecting seeds from this year's crop ensures a crop for the next season. The seeds are carefully stored for planting next spring. Therefore, harvesting also requires forethought and planning for harvests to come. The harvest is not just consuming—it also entails setting a portion aside for the future. Today's gardener has come to rely on seed companies to do this task. Admittedly, this simplifies things. It also removes a key step in the process that, in turn, removes part of our understanding and meaning of gardening. It gives us pause to ponder what other aspects of our lives have been "removed" or "taken care of" by someone or something else.

There is a subtle yet sublime joy the gardener experiences during harvest. Sometimes it is immediate delight of picking a strawberry or tomato straight from the plant and eating it right then and there. It might be at the dinner table as part of a complete meal. There is a tangible outcome representing all the time and effort that went into this blissful moment that sustains us by feeding the body *and* soul. In some ways, harvesting a garden is analogous to any craft—woodworking, quilting, restoring a classic car. Upon completion, you can stand back and admire your handy work. The difference with gardening is this moment of satisfaction can be fleeting. We consume the product instead of displaying or using it. But this consumption actually fulfills us and sustains us to keep us going. And the gardener knows that while the season may have come to an end, the garden itself is not over. The whole wonderful (as in full of wonder) process will repeat itself in the coming year, a realization that nourishes body and soul.

In some ways, harvest embodies truth. Gardeners cannot "fake" their work or work half-heartedly. If they do, the truth of their effort reveals itself in what is produced in that plot of soil. It is how they practice gardening that results in what is (or isn't) harvested. If the garden fails, the gardener cannot blame the actions or efforts of someone else. It is what it is. Conversely, the gardener can take great pride in what does grow and blossom. Ultimately, the end result sustains the gardener physically and spiritually.

We must remember that our holiday of Thanksgiving is a celebration of the harvest. Families and friends came together to enjoy not only each other, but to enjoy the result of their hard work in the garden. They came together to *give thanks* for what they had worked so hard to produce. Sadly, we may have forgotten the essence of that celebration, partly because most of us no longer take an active role in producing the food we eat. If our livelihood depended on what we grew, you can bet that we would express our gratitude for what came up out of the ground. Regardless of a national holiday on the fourth Thursday of November, gardeners celebrate their own mini-Thanksgiving each time they bite into produce picked moments ago. It's sad that so many people have never experienced such a simple joy.

Essentially, we get out of it what we put into it. The joy and reward that is derived from the harvest is the direct result of tending to the garden. As we have seen from previous pages and passages, it doesn't just happen. When we bite into that tomato, we are biting into the earth, sun, water that went into it and subsequently into us. We are intimately connected to God's creation.

Many people no longer appreciate where food comes from. We live in a society of convenience where some unknown persons produce our produce for us. It has become a matter of accenting which syllable in the word. At best, we've become dependent upon huge agribusiness farms to provide for us and at worst, we've absolved ourselves from any responsibility for sustaining and nurturing our self.

Perhaps the same can be said for our spirituality and daily lives. We have come to expect someone or something—a pastor, congregation, career, a "big box" store—to produce and feed us our "soul food" on our behalf just as we expect a gardener or grocer to produce the food that sustains us. We wait for "it" to happen or appear. There is little wonder that many do not understand what spirituality is or how to cultivate it, just as so few of us don't understand or practice gardening. Hopefully this little book has shed some light.

We often go to church to pick up some soul food much in the same way we go to the store to pick up a plastic bag of prepared salad. That works, of course, but only to degree. The depth of our understanding and appreciation is limited. It leads us to wonder what it is being harvested from our lives? What am I getting from my job? My relationships? The way I spend my time? These questions are deep and, at times, frightening to ponder. They are the barometers of meaning and purpose.

The garden mirrors our spirituality. It requires tending by devoting time, attention, thought, and action that produce something that can be harvested to sustain us. We gain insight and derive the underlying meaning of what goes into something when we are intimately engaged and involved in the process. Each of us has experienced this revelation upon completion of a new and challenging activity. We come to know and understand what it takes to accomplish that task. We discover what it means to engage in that activity. We have a deeper appreciation because we were a part of it and it became a part of us. Scholar Elizabeth Tisdell defined spirituality as "a way of life that affects and includes every moment of existence. It is at once a contemplative attitude, a disposition to a life of depth, and the search for ultimate meaning, direction, and belonging. The spiritual person is committed to *growth* as an essential ongoing life goal" (pp. 17-18). Growth—a key word that resonates with the gardener.

As joyful as the harvest is, the gardener knows this bounty is both temporary and ongoing. The act of gathering produce has a beginning and an end. At some point, there simply aren't any crops left to gather. Likewise, the gardener knows deep inside that harvest actually takes place in different ways during different parts of the seasons. Walking through or sitting in a garden at any time of the year—not just during harvest season—provides a harvest for the senses. Noticing the smells, sights, and sounds is a harvest in and of itself that feeds the soul. The whole process of planting, tending, and gathering must repeat itself with and through the seasons. But this revelation that the gathering is only temporarily complete is not necessarily sad. In fact, it is full of hope.

Reflection

What is an aspect of your life that you have had to intentionally tend to? What was the end result of your effort and how did you feel?

What feeds your soul? Where and when do you find it?

Have you come to expect everything in your life to be cosmetically perfect? Why or why not? How realistic is that? What are the pros and cons of such an expectation or desire?

What are some examples of "volunteer plants" that have unexpectedly sprung up in your life? What emotions did this evoke?

Harvest embodies truth. To what extent does the way you live your life embody truth, and what is that truth? Conversely, in what ways do you "fake" your way through life?

How often do you celebrate the bounty of your life? How do you express that gratitude?

Do you know where your food comes from (other than the supermarket)? Why would that matter, if at all?

Do you depend on someone or something like a pastor or congregation to provide for your spiritual needs the same way you depend on the grocer to provide your food? If so, what are the ramifications of that?

Tips for Cultivating Your Spirituality

Walk through, or sit in, a garden or vineyard. Take it all in. Listen to your inner thoughts. Revel in the quiet and sounds, the smells, and the colors. Just "be there" for a few moments. If it is winter and the garden is put to bed, contemplate the rest it deserves and celebrate all it has provided.

Notice what you "harvest" from tending to the important things in your life. Ponder what went into this effort and what came from it.

Continue to be a member of a community of faith. Consider other ways to harvest the bounty of sharing through study groups or volunteering.

Don't wait for Thanksgiving to celebrate the bounty of your life. Gather friends and family to share a meal and celebrate how you nurture each other's lives.

If you don't have a garden, or if you only have a small or limited garden, go to a farmer's market to supplement what you've grown. This allows you to eat locally grown food and to meet the gardener who gave you this wonderful food. This simple act of eating locally grown produce feeds your soul as you have a deeper understanding and appreciation of where and how the food was produced rather than picking it up off a refrigerated bin at a supermarket. It just may be healthier, too.

Start your own community garden at your church. Consult the final chapter of this book to learn more.

Prayer

Gracious God—

Thank you for your creation that abundantly provides for us. The garden is your temple where we can find you and where you can find us. We recognize that what we harvest embodies truth. Give us the strength and resources to tend to the garden so we might be true to you and to ourselves.

Amen

Chapter 14

To Everything . . . . Seasons

Seedling for Thought

Spring passes and one remembers one's innocence. Summer passes and one remembers one's exuberance. Autumn passes and one remembers one's reverence. Winter passes and one remembers one's perseverance.

~ Yoko Ono

Scripture

Ecclesiastes 3
There is a time for everything and a season for every activity under the heavens.

*   *   *

Every gardener understands what each season brings to the garden. Spring, of course, is a time of eternal hope and optimism of things to come. Nature is coming back to life after being dormant. The light has changed—days are getting longer and warmer. Consequently, many inexperienced gardeners are inspired to begin planting seeds and small tomato seedlings at these first hints of spring. It is typically the warm and sunny Saturday after a long, dark, and cold winter that sends eager urban farmers to the garden center where gardening supplies are on display. They enthusiastically plant their seeds and seedlings only to have them nipped by a late spring frost. The seasoned gardener knows when the last day of frost is likely for the region and waits ever so patiently, resisting that urge to plant. Instead, the plots in the garden are prepared. And when the last day of potential frost has come and gone, gardeners are on their hands and knees digging in the dirt in what is no less a posture of prayer than any other devout person kneeling in a grand cathedral. It is prayer of hope and thanks. Spring is a time for rebirth and renewal.

Summer is when the garden and gardener are most alive. Seeds and seedlings have taken root. These fledgling plants grow expanding and filling the spaces that were marked out in the spring. The once empty and sparse garden is now full and crowded with abundance. Summer is a time for labor of love. Mulching, weeding, watering, and staking are required. Each task requires effort but is no less gratifying than the energy we expend in tending to anything worthy of our time and attention. Fingernails seemed to be forever caked with dirt. Stained calluses on the hands are indicative of work.

The shorter and cooler days of fall bring harvest. The gardener is able to reap the rewards of their labor. The produce is gathered and stored. We are sustained not only by consuming the food, but by the act of harvesting as well. Our souls and our stomachs are fed. In the process, the gardener begins to notice the subtle indicators of the garden's decline. Less and less is produced. More and more space opens up as plants are removed from the garden bed. The daylight is changing, and shadows creep earlier and longer from the southwest. Initially, it may appear to be a time of sadness. In reality, fall brings reflection as well as appreciation. It allows us to ponder not only on what is, but also on what has been. Fall brings gratitude for what we have been given. Not so long ago, fall meant canning and storing produce to be consumed during the winter. Even the process of storing food was actually connected to earth as the homes had below ground fruit cellars where the natural cool temperature safely prolonged the life of the harvested produce.

The gardener essentially puts the garden to bed in the winter. The darkness of the season provides the much deserved and needed rest for the spent soil. Snow blankets the ground. Walking through the garden at this time of year provides a different kind of quiet and peace. Everything is still. And while the garden rests, the gardener thumbs through seed and garden supply catalogues in anticipation of the cycle beginning once again.

The seasons of the garden are a metaphor for the transitions in our own lives. It provides an opportunity to take note and celebrate the birth, growth, blossom, and decline of phases and events we experience. When we fret and worry about any particular stage, we can take comfort in the fact we are in a particular season, and a new cycle waits for us to tend to it, just like a new season of gardening. Childhood has its own season, as does adolescence, young adulthood, mid-life, and the golden years. The garden reminds us of the seasons of life in a whirlwind world where we are often too busy to take note of natural cycles and rhythms. So much of what we see, feel, hear, and do are artificially constructed. We are removed from God's creation and therefore removed from what it has to give and teach us. Our existence takes place in "seasonally controlled" work places. We hurl through space and time as passers-by cocooned in vehicles. And if we notice anything seasonal while in motion, it is usually how the rain or snow has inconvenienced our commute. When and if we do walk, we blot out the world with ear pods looking down at a digital device intended to provide information at the expense of the knowledge the natural world provides. Working in the garden means getting dirty and ruining $50 manicures.

Long ago, in agricultural times, we not only took note of the seasons, we celebrated them. The solstice and equinox were transitions of what needed to be done to plant, grow, harvest, and store our food. The early church deliberately shifted attention from these pagan celebrations that honored something other than God to historical events and metaphors in Christianity. In some respects, we're in danger of losing our wonder and awe of God's natural creation. And even these new seasonal celebrations intended to redirect our affections and attention to God have been subverted into commercial enticements of a replacement religion of consumerism and materialism. Easter is now about chocolate bunnies rather than new life springing from the dead. Rather than giving thanks for bounty, Thanksgiving is about food binges and football. One minute after midnight, Black Friday launches us into a season of consumer frenzy in which we lose sight of the true purpose and metaphor of Christ's birth as a light in a season of darkness.

Perhaps the most significant example of being out of sync with the seasons is the manner of what and when we eat. Many of us have grown accustomed to eating out of season. We have forgotten that tomatoes come in the summer. We no longer eagerly await the first sweet strawberries of the season. In a sense, we have become seasonally and agriculturally ignorant while removing our selves from any interaction or relationship with produce. Hothouses that extend or artificially create the necessary growing conditions of certain crops create the illusion of "season-less-ness." Shipping produce from anywhere in the world plants a seed of entitlement to eat any fruit or vegetable whenever we want. We ship our desires from the southern hemisphere at great expense, both financially and environmentally, to stock our shelves and fill our stomachs with out-of-season treats. But these desires and behaviors are really only symptoms of something deeper.

It all began in the garden. This is where we found God. We've suggested on these pages that returning to or at least visiting the garden is a way to feed your soul. We've also proposed that in many ways tending the garden is much like tending our spiritual lives. So even if you don't have a plot of earth to tend, we invite you to dig deep into your own life, and see what abundance you can harvest.

Reflection

What is your favorite season and why?

What does each season represent or symbolize to you?

What season is your life in right now?

Do you note or celebrate the transition of seasons? If so, how? If not, why?

Have you thought about what you eat and when you eat it? Do you eat tomatoes in the winter? If so, how does what you eat get to your plate?

Tips for Cultivating Your Spirituality

If you don't have a garden, consider joining a community-supported agriculture (CSA) group. You pay a "subscription" to receive garden produce each week. Through your weekly delivery, you will begin to notice seasonality of food. Review the next section of this book to learn how to start a community garden at your own church.

Keep a journal or just a diary of events. Using the seasonal transitions of the solstices and equinoxes as a cue, review your entries to see what characterized that season of your life.

Make a timeline of your life divided up into decades. Chart/mark/list events. Reflect on the nature of those events and how they may reflect the various "seasons of your life."

Make a timeline of Christ's life and ministry and categorize the "seasons" of his ministry.

Spirituality is cultivating relationships with yourself, others, and God. Look at the "seasons" of your relationships.

Ponder the true meaning and message of Christian seasonal celebration. Intentionally set aside time to read about and celebrate Christ's birth, Epiphany, Lent, Easter, and Pentecost. Consider how to have special meal symbolizing and celebrating those seasons.

Prayer

Gracious God—
Thank you for the light and new birth that comes with spring—a time of hope. Thank you for the warmth that summer brings—a time for work and play. Thank you for the bounty and harvest that comes with the autumn of

our lives—a time for reflection and celebration. Thank you for the rest that soothes our tired souls, bodies, and minds during the darkness of winter—a time to be still and know you.

Amen

PART II

Starting a Church Community Garden

Together with a handful of friends from our congregation, we created a very simple, straightforward community garden at our own church. When we say "simple" and "straightforward" we mean we started with a good idea, willing and interested friends, and virtually no budget. We share this to illustrate that starting a community garden at a church does not have to be as difficult or challenging as one might think. Over a decade, our garden, known as *Stewardship on Urban Land* or S.O.U.L (where we grew "soul food"), blossomed in more ways than one.

It started in an unused two acre area behind the church with a handful of 15 x 15 foot plots and expanded to two dozen 20 X 20 plots, a collection of raised beds among paved pathways for seniors with limited mobility, and a small rustic labyrinth made from un-used bricks. We established a "serenity corner" with benches for those seeking silent mediation. This area holds a special place in our heart and memory, as it was also the venue of our son and daughter-in-law's wedding reception. Anyone could have a plot, even folks who were not members of the congregation, if they agreed to a few basic guidelines. This included a willingness to "tithe" a portion of their produce each week to be sold after each Sunday service. All proceeds from the free-will offering taken from the sale of the produce went directly to a local agency dealing with hunger issues. We begin this section of this book with this brief history as a context for our own experience and an invitation to your community of faith. The ideas, guidelines, and suggestions presented here came out of our decade-long adventure in church community gardening.

Site—There's lots to think about when choosing a site. Starting with the basics, consider how much sun the site will receive, a minimum of 6-8 hours in the summer. Then, think about water—access to it and getting it to your crops, as well as how much it will cost. A flat site is ideal, as it will minimize water run off. But if that is not possible, consider using raised beds on terraced slopes. Believe it or not, some cities have "beauty ordinances" that may actually prohibit gardens because they are "agricultural" and MAY be viewed as a visual blight—and no, we're not kidding. So, you might want to check before you put a lot of time, work, and money into a garden plot.

Proposal, Permission & Approval—You can't just start digging up the church lawn to start a garden. A good way to start is to submit a written a proposal to your church's governing body. The proposal should be simple and straightforward using the "5W's"—WHO is proposing to do WHAT, WHERE, WHEN and WHY. List and name the coordinators or leaders who will oversee the operation of the garden. Indicate what the purpose of the garden is, as well as what particular site is being proposed. Also include a list of materials or equipment that will be needed initially. A modest budget should also be proposed. As stated in the preface to this section, our initial garden operation had NO budget. We collected a small operation fund by charging a fee of $15 for each gardener. This allowed us to purchase hoses and other basic equipment, while individual gardeners provided their own tools while working in their own plot. Consider suggesting that the garden coordinators "report" to the Building and Grounds or Mission Committees for proper oversight. The proposal should include timeline for when the garden operation would begin, including organizational meetings, actual preparation of the plot, periodic oversight meetings, and the intended life of the garden. The last section on a rationale should incorporate language that reflects the mission of the church. Our original intent was to provide fresh produce to local food shelters. However, we quickly learned this was not feasible. We did not have enough quantities of produce or the means to transport the produce on a daily basis. Furthermore, many of the local food banks and pantries did not even have the capacity to refrigerate and store fresh produce. As a result, we modified our "mission" by collecting approximately 10% of ready produce from each garden plot every Sunday morning to be sold to our congregation immediately after worship service during coffee hour with a free-will offering. We took turns staffing the Sunday morning market. We collected the proceeds and donated 100% of the funds to a local hunger agency. The congregation benefitted from fresh, organic produce and the community received much needed financial assistance.

Budget—Start modestly. We acquired many of our building materials through Craigslist, Freecycle, or donated by church members with spare items, like lumber for garden bed borders. A local tree service in need of some place to dump wood chips provided our walkway mulch. A church member who was a landscaper brought untreated grass clippings (no Weed 'N Feed) and leaves for the compost piles. He also donated a couple of old lawn mowers. Sod for a grassy area for picnics and gatherings were provided by a couple that tore out their lawn and replaced it with xeriscape design. The buildings and grounds operating budget of the church included water costs.

Water—Small individual plots can be hand watered, which conserves water by targeting the soil around each plant. Sprinkling has a high evaporation rate and is not good for plants because fungi and viruses can easily spread. Snails and slugs also like everything wet. Drip irrigation is higher end, more costly and time-intensive to set up, but saves water and keeps plants healthy. Years before, we hauled water in 5 gallon buckets from a shared, communal spigot at a community garden while in graduate school which worked fine and kept us in shape. You are intimately aware of your plants' growth in this way.

Organizational meeting & orientation—It is very important to meet with potential gardeners so that everyone understands the expectations of garden membership. The amount of community work, tithing of produce, watering procedures, prohibition of synthetic fertilizers and pesticides, and tidiness are all important for the group to have consensus on. The members should sign a **Covenant** in which they agree to weed the pathway(s) around their plot, use organic and sustainable gardening practices, and take care of common areas. Some gardens require a definite number of hours to be worked in the common areas, others adopt an area and care for it (the berry patch, asparagus patch, herb beds, flower borders, grassy picnic area, etc.). The group should decide how best to meet the garden's ever demanding needs.

Pathways & Plots—Our paths were 4' wide and mulched with cardboard and wood chips. Bike shops are a great place to obtain BIG cardboard boxes that are just about four feet weed and seven feet long—be sure to remove copper staples from the cardboard before laying it down. The paths surrounded four 15 x 15 plots within a section in order to access an individual garden plot from two sides. Individuals created walkways and sub plots in their 15 x 15 plot. We later enlarged them to 20x20 spaces for slightly more produce space in the sub plots. This also required reconfiguring the pathways, as we wanted to maintain the 4' wide pathways to accommodate wheelbarrows and our garden cart. Some people chose to build raised beds, and in many areas, this is a wise choice. Gardeners can also attach hardware cloth to the bottom of raised beds to prevent gophers and other critters from tunneling into the beds. The soil in the raised beds warms up more quickly in the spring, and watering can be controlled more easily. Raised beds that are three feet high can also provide easier access for the elderly or disabled. Our church had a day care operation for the elderly with dementia. Part of their day included a trip out on the brick paved walkways to putter in their raised garden beds. This is an easy and beneficial church youth group or scout project.

Shed/storage & tools—Chances are the church already has storage facilities for yard upkeep equipment. Check to see if the garden can store some of its equipment in the same storage area. A locked shed on site is a convenient option for storing wheelbarrows, hoses, rakes, shovels, weed eaters, and other common tools. Our shed was a renovated railroad caboose! A tiller was purchased through a special grant from the church.

Dues/fees—Calculate your basic annual costs (primarily water + supplies hoses, wheelbarrows, etc.) and divide by number of gardeners. We had fifteen gardeners who paid $15 a year dues. We were fortunate to have water subsidized by the church as the property provided an easement for a county water canal and a reduced water rate in return. Many community gardens charge $40 or more to offset water expenses. The return on these fees, however, is very high and fairly quick.

Security & Issues—Along with fencing for wildlife, you may need to consider fencing to prevent stealing, and vandalism. Halloween time was particularly vulnerable as our pumpkins often "disappeared." Once in a while, neighbors just sort of wandered in and "borrowed" things assuming it was a "community garden" for the neighborhood. A parking lot light fixture at night may help as well, although consider nocturnal wildlife needs. Owls hunt at night and can be an important piece of integrated pest management.

Fencing—This is specific to your area. Do you have deer? Rabbits? Gophers? Consider the wildlife that want to share your produce as its own personal salad bar when you decide upon fencing.

Soil—Wise farmers say that they are not raising healthy plants; they are really nurturing healthy, active life in the soil. Increasing the microbiological activity promote healthy plants that can withstand pests, diseases and weather problems. Compost, sheet mulch, addition of slow release organic fertilizers, composted manure, green manures, double digging, and crop rotation are all methods of increasing the tilth, life and health of the soil. Chances are, you will have garden members who are skilled in these areas. If not, your local master gardeners, community college, or nurseries will have classes in basic gardening practices. It could even be a service-learning class project from a nearby high school or college class.

Coordinators—We had two individuals and two couples to share the responsibilities such as assign plots, collect fees, gather tithing and sell produce. Work with building and grounds committee to identify a point person to deal with infrastructure and maintenance issues such as irrigation leaks.

Gatherings—Social gatherings are also important. We combined communal work and potluck meals referring to them as "Munch and Mulch" or "Weed and Feed" parties. In November, we also had a harvest celebration in the form of a soup luncheon in our fellowship hall after the worship service. People brought their favorite homemade soup, bread or dessert to share, in celebration of a wonderful harvest from the garden. A free-will offering was gathered with small proceeds going to support the garden, but the bulk of the donations went to a local food bank.

Tithing + free will offerings + community partners. The Biblical practice of tithing was practiced in our garden as well. As noted before, we harvested approximately 10% from each plot on Saturday night or Sunday morning and held a little farmer's market after each service. Members of the church gave free will donations for the produce, 100% of which went to agreed-upon local hunger programs supported by the church. Members who could not garden, such as the elderly or those living in apartments, had access to very fresh, local, healthy produce while supporting hunger programs. The garden produced abundantly and we were able to share its bounty with so many members, and extend that bounty to the greater community

Wrapping Up

We've shared our own experience with you here. This is enough to get you started. We also know there is much more information on the web. Here are a few websites on other church gardens.

- http://blog.mlive.com/grpress/2008/06/church_gardens_build_community.htm

- http://www.mennoweekly.org/2009/8/24/church-gardens-growing-trend/
- http://www.emmitsburg.net/gardens/articles/adams/2007/church_gardens.htm
- http://abclocal.go.com/wtvd/story?section=news/local&id=6810433

We hope you can see how much joy the church garden brought to us, our fellow gardeners, the congregation as a whole, and to the community at-large. Thanks for reading our little book on how to tend your spirituality as well as your garden. For more information, go to our own website, SPIRITUALITY FOR TODAY at http://spiritualityfortoday.webs.com. We hope you have harvested a few things that will feed your soul. Blessings!

References and Notes

Introduction

Sam Hamilton-Poore (2005). The given and the gift: sexuality and God's eros in spiritual direction and supervision. In M.R. Bumpus & R.B. Langer (Eds.), *Supervision of spiritual directors: Engaging the Holy mystery* (pp. 83-104). Harrisburg, PA: Morehouse Press

Chapter 3

California Master Gardener Handbook (2002). Edited by, Dennis R. Pitteneger. University of California Agricultural and Natural Resources.

A Woman's Hardy Garden (1990). Helena Rutherford Ely. New York: Collier Books.

Chapter 4

Sabbath: Finding Rest, Renewal, and Delight In Our Busy Lives (1999). Wayne Mueller. New York: Bantam Books.

Chapter 5

Bio-spirituality: Focusing As A Way To Grow (1997). Peter A. Campbell and Edwin M. McMahon. Chicago: Loyola Press.

Chapter 7

Saint Ignatius of Loyola Personal Writings (1996). New York: Penguin Press.

Chapter 8

U.S. Department of Agriculture—Natural Resource Conservation Services. *Mulching for Moisture, Weed Control, and Soil Protection* (USDA NRCS Practice 484). ftp://ftp-fc.sc.egov.usda.gov/HI/pub/technical/conservation_system/CSG_Mulching_484.pdf

Chapter 9

A History of Christian Spirituality: An Analytical Introduction (2002). Urban T. Holmes. New York: Morehouse Publishing.

Chapter 10

University of Illinois Extension Office. *Composting for the Home Owner.* http://web.extension.illinois.edu/homecompost/history.html

Chapter 11

Online Etymological Dictionary. http://www.etymonline.com/*Holy Listening: The Art of Spiritual Direction* (1992). Margaret Guenther. Cambridge, MA: Cowley Publications.

A Sacred Voice is Calling: Personal Vocation and Social Conscience (2006). John Neafsey. Maryknoll, NY: Orbis Books.

Chapter 13

Exploring spirituality and culture in adult and higher education (2003). Elizabeth Tisdell. San Francisco: Jossey-Bass.

About the Authors

Marshall Welch is currently the Director of the Catholic Institute for Lasallian Social Action (CILSA) at Saint Mary's College of California where he oversees service-learning and social justice courses. He has a Ph.D. in Special Education and has been in higher education since 1987 as a faculty member and director of service-learning programs. Marshall is also a Commissioned Lay Pastor (CLP) in the Presbyterian USA church. He earned his Diploma of Arts in Spiritual Direction and Doctor of Ministry and San Francisco Theological Seminary. Marshall is a Spiritual Director and conducts spiritual direction with individuals and small groups with an emphasis in nurturing men's spirituality. He also facilitates innovative workshops and classes using the music of U2, Paul Simon, and Johnny Cash as well as contemporary movies to explore spiritual formation.

Julie Welch has a Masters degree in Therapeutic Recreation and is a certified special education teacher. She worked at rehabilitation centers and then spent 14 years working with junior high students who have severe disabilities. Julie took a lead role in creating a community garden at their church while living in Salt Lake City. Julie now spends her time as a nature and garden education specialist. She splits her time as the steward of the Legacy Garden at Saint Mary's College of California and working with local schools and community gardens. She is a certified Master Gardener in the State of California and teaches a course on "low-impact" living. Together with Marshall, they have led workshops and courses on "deeper living in a shallow world" to promote a more sustainable and intentional lifestyle.

Marshall and Julie conduct workshops on spiritual formation and community gardening.

Edwards Brothers Malloy
Thorofare, NJ USA
April 19, 2013